# The West Riding of Yorkshire in 1842

## The Landscape Histories

Editor: Peter Lavery

Warwickshire in 1790
The West Riding of Yorkshire in 1842
Sussex in 1839
Surrey in 1815
Lancashire in 1648
Essex in 1603
Norfolk and Suffolk in 1733
Bedfordshire and Buckinghamshire in 1720

Harold Speak and Jean Forrester

# The West Riding of Yorkshire in 1842

OSPREY

Published in 1974 by
Osprey Publishing Ltd., P.O. Box 25
707 Oxford Road, Reading, Berkshire



ISBN 0 85045 178 7

Filmset and printed by
BAS Printers Limited, Wallop, Hampshire



# Contents

# 1. Landscape and agriculture

2. Todmorden from the North. A typical Pennine landscape on the borders of Lancashire and Yorkshire. The steep hill roads made it necessary for farm carts to climb on a zigzag course.

The summer of 1842 was the hottest and driest within living memory. In the countryside the fields were parched. Hundreds of the rivulets which fed the fan-like river network of Yorkshire were dry gullies or little more than trickles of water. On 26 June a hurricane did considerable damage to fruit trees at Barnsley. In the heat the unsanitary towns reeked with offensive smells. Many mills were idle; poverty and unemployment were rife; riots and strikes occurred; the military was alerted; the prisons overflowed. Yet despite this distress the middle classes continued to attend balls and the hunt, and the aristocracy to enjoy the comforts of wealth and privilege in their stately homes.

In many ways it was a year when trade and time stood still; a breathing space, perhaps, before mechanization and modernization galloped on to destroy the last of old Yorkshire, now overlaid uneasily by the new. In the valleys of the Aire and Calder and southwards to Sheffield and Rotherham, ancient settlements and rural hamlets had grown, unplanned, into teeming towns and industrial villages, with dozens of industries based on coal, iron and textiles.

A traveller entering the county from the south along the Great North Road, via Doncaster, would see little of this development, but if he came from Lancashire in the west along the Calder Valley it would extend all

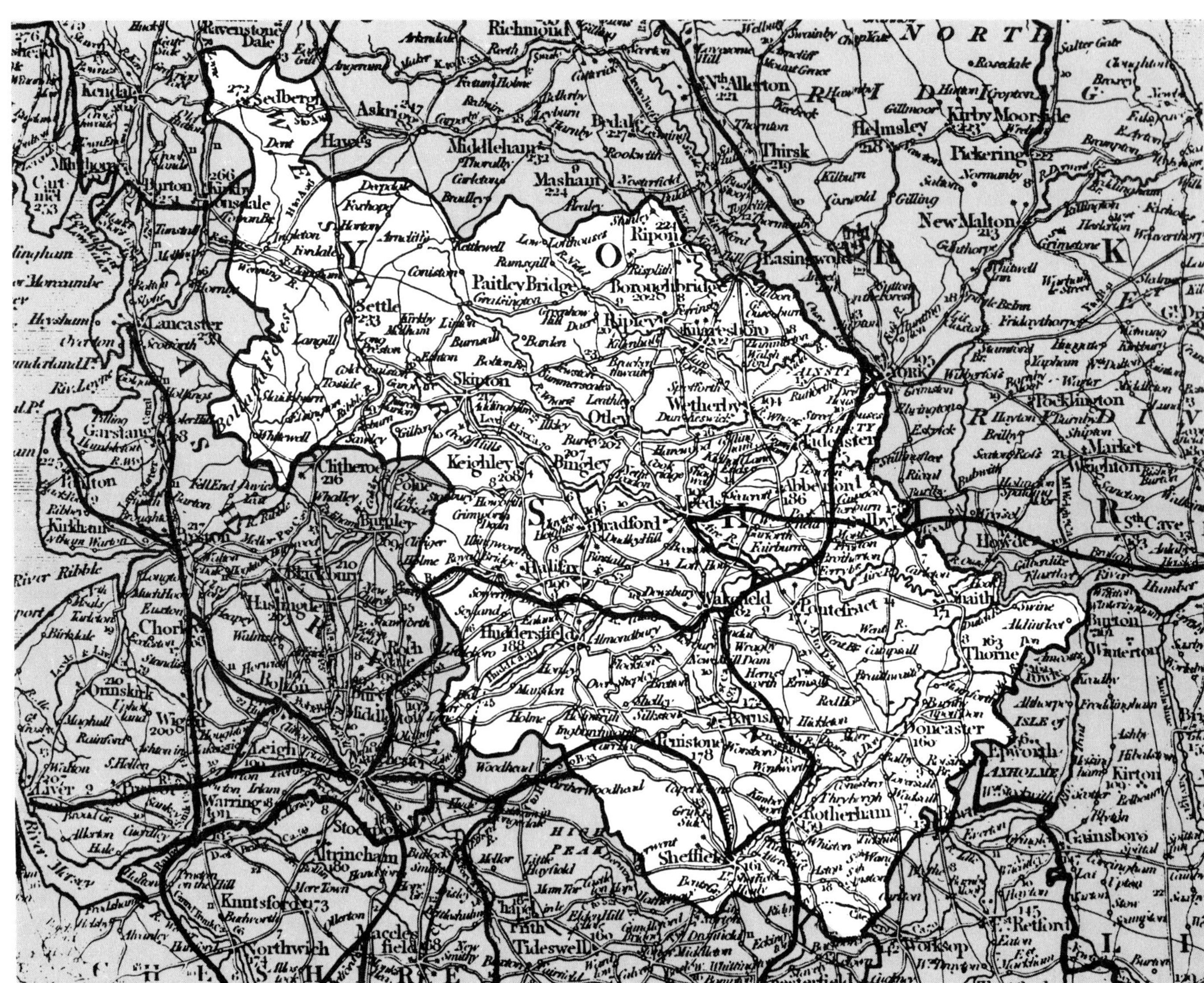


1. The West Riding area, from Cary's Map of England and Wales, corrected to the year 1841, and showing the railways.

around him. Standing on the high bleak summit of Standedge, the very backbone of the Pennines, he could see on a clear day a great expanse of Lancashire and beyond to the hills of Cheshire and Derbyshire, and as far as the mountains of Wales. To the east were the craggy, barren hilltops, the vast peat moors and the deep winding valleys of Yorkshire. Below him lay the newly-opened Manchester to Leeds Railway, stretching like a silver thread to link the commerce and industry of Lancashire and Yorkshire in an ever increasing flow of men and merchandise.

When the section from Hebden Bridge to Normanton was opened on 5 October 1840, thousands had lined the hillsides to watch the first train go by. What a bewildering sight it must have been, for many of those watching had never ventured far from their hillside homes, where they lived in isolated farms or small communities as their fathers had done for centuries, seeing little of the outside world. Henry Clarkson of Wakefield, who surveyed part of the line for the great engineer George Stephenson, had travelled for miles through this rough hill country to find the owners of parcels of land required by the railway company. He recounted that often people were not known by their surnames but were called after their father – Bill o' Jack's, or Tom o' Dick's. Of the people he wrote: 'The physical character of the inhabitants of these valleys was for the most part uncouth and strange, in keeping with the roughness of their speech and manners.'

Below Eastwood Station the railway, turnpike road and canal, confined by the narrowness of the valley, formed parallel routes linking the two counties. Cobbett considered this the most interesting part of England that he ever saw, with never-ending chains of hillocks, the deep valleys in the hills, every one with its stream of clear water. Farther east, at Mytholm, the railway crossed riverside meadows which were interspersed with cotton and woollen mills and houses of the

3. A pastoral scene overlooking Sowerby Bridge. The increasing population of the industrial areas provided good markets for local farmers.

4. Brighouse. Resting farmworkers look down upon the mills in the valley.

local gentry. Workers' cottages were built on the hill-sides. The line passed on to Hebden Bridge, a little town of about 1,500 people with scenery which had been compared with the Highlands of Scotland. In the surrounding hills were the isolated homes of the hill farmers who for centuries had eked out the meagre living they won from the land by spinning and weaving in their homes. The local buildings had especially long windows to provide the last glimmer of light for the worker at the loom.

Two and a half miles north of the beautiful and ancient village of Elland was the growing town of Halifax. Next came Brighouse, one of the more important stations on the line, notable for buildings constructed in a distinctive Chinese style. Bradford was only seven miles away and nearer still was the great iron and coal works on Wibsey Low Moor. Through Cooper Bridge, Mirfield and Hopton the new line ran to Dewsbury, and then on to Horbury. High embankments carried the railway along the edge of the flood plain of the Calder at Lupset Pastures. On the opposite side lay millions of tons of gravel, the floor of a post-glacial lake, the newer soils upon them forming rich flat meadows. At Wakefield the railway took its course through a deep cutting, in the face of which coal seams were visible. It then crossed the Calder and, leaving the valley, completed its journey at Normanton.

In the nineteenth century most of the development in the West Riding was taking place on the coal measures, comprising an area from the north of Leeds southwards to the borders of Derbyshire, and from the summit of the Pennines in the west to the beginning of the magnesian limestone in the east. In addition to coal- and iron-bearing rocks and an abundance of running water, the region provided ample building materials, stone, clay and wood, with which to erect the many new mills and factories and the thousands of humble dwellings for the fast-growing population. In the hillier parts of the Pennines, especially, the sandstones of the middle coal measures provided the staple building material, so that structures looked as strong and enduring as the rugged hills around them. On the lower slopes of the hills and where the valleys widened, as at Wakefield and Leeds, hand-made bricks were also used, sometimes encasing the timber frames of earlier structures.

Overlying the coal measures to the east, a band of magnesian limestone, about twelve miles wide, runs across the county from north to south, separating the Pennine country from the flat lands of the Vale of York and Hatfield Chase. Another limestone, the carboniferous, gives to the Pennines north of Leeds a character different from that of the gritstone to the south. Each of these regions had its own characteristic features and consequent human activities, and there are few places in the world with such variety of geology and scenery in so small an area.

A chronicler of the period said that farms in the West Riding were generally small, but agricultural improvements had been extensive and 'every species of amelioration of the soil which industry, skill and capital can accomplish has been brought into action; especially during the present century, in which the greater part of the common and waste lands have been enclosed and cultivated.'

In a county of such varied topography, farming varied too. East of Leeds, Wakefield and Sheffield were the rolling cornlands providing the staple food for the industrial population. Flax, teazels and dyer's woad (*Isatis tinctoria*) were grown on the marsh lands near Cawood, Sherburn, Snaith and Thorne. On the rich warp lands bordering the Ouse near Goole and Swinefleet potatoes were an important crop, yielding on average seventy sacks to the acre, and on good soil as much as one hundred sacks. Woad, used as a foundation colour in dyeing cloth, was grown with barley or clover, sometimes as a separate crop. At Pontefract liquorice, reputedly introduced by the monks in the Middle Ages, grew in the rich deep soil, and Pomfret cakes, made from its juices, were a local speciality. Chicory (recently introduced) and mustard were

5. Malham Cove: magnificent scenery in the limestone area in the north-west of the West Riding – the area is a geologist's paradise. The River Aire rises here.

6. Walton Hall, near Wakefield, the home of the celebrated naturalist, Charles Waterton. It was here that he made the first nature reserve in the world.

grown near York; peas, beans and turnips were familiar crops.

Recently William Cobbett had travelled by road from Todmorden to Leeds via Halifax and Bradford, and recorded that the adjoining region was the poorest country he had ever set his eyes on except for 'that miserable Nova Scotia', thickly populated and producing nothing but the natural grass of the country which, although 'not bad', was all needed to produce milk for the immense population covering the whole face of the country. The only grain crop he saw was one of very poor oats, with sheaves no more than a foot and a half high.

Much of the north-western part of the West Riding was grazing land for thousands of cattle and sheep. In the Craven area there were long-horned cattle of a hardy breed well suited to the climate. At other places, as in Nidderdale, they had been crossed with the short-horned cattle from Holderness in the East Riding, which were said to fatten quicker and more cheaply. Many different breeds of sheep were found, in most places so cross-bred that they could not be distinguished. Others had been improved by the introduction of Leicestershire sheep thirty years earlier. Most of the mountain sheep of the western Pennines were black-faced, and they had long legs which fitted them admirably for their hilly pastures.

Improvements to the land had been made possible by the earlier enclosures, and farmers and landowners were concerned with bettering their consolidated holdings. Draining and fertilization were the main topics of the day, and the journal of the recently established Royal Agricultural Society of England and the *Gardener's Chronicle* circulated much valuable information to farmers. The Lord Lieutenant, Lord Wharncliffe, was President of the Yorkshire Agricultural Society; and local societies were formed soon afterwards, as at Wakefield where the Wakefield Farmers' Club was formed in November 1842.

In January of that year, the Yorkshire Land-drainage Association had been proposed. Drainage greatly improved the value and productivity of the land. The older method of filling a trench with stone, topped with straw, was giving way to a new method using tile drains placed at an average distance of seven yards apart. In those parts of the West Riding where clay and coal were plentiful, these tiles cost about 18*s*. per 1000. Improvement in profits due to well-drained soil varied between 20 and 100 per cent. Experiments showed that drained and manured land gave 36 bushels of wheat to the acre, as against 22 bushels for undrained manured land. In the south-east the low flat land of Hatfield Chase was now rich farmland, its drainage supervised by a Court of Sewers.

The farmers of the day had calculated the difference in time and manpower for working different kinds of soil. On dry land a man and two horses could plough the same extent in the same time as a man and a boy with three horses on a clay field.

Lime from the magnesian limestone belt was conveyed by cart, barge and rail to the areas of heavy clay soil, where its value as a fertilizer was well known. Guano, then imported from South America, was regarded as the perfect manure. In 1842, J. B. Laws patented the first successful chemical manures at Rothamstead. Elsewhere others were trying out various compounds, and Henry Briggs of Overton, near Wakefield, claimed that if farmers put back into the soil each year the particular chemicals extracted by the previous crop, they would no longer be tied to the rotation of crops, but could grow, year after year, the crop best suited to their land. He recommended a fertilizer made up of the following quantities of ingredients per acre:

| | | | |
|---|---|---|---|
| Potash | 6lb. | magnesia | 3½lb. |
| soda | 6½lb. | sulphuric acid | 2¾lb. |
| chlorine | 1½lb. | phosphoric acid | 8¾lb. |
| lime | 12¾lb. | farmyard manure | 1 ton |

Nitrogen would be provided from the manure and phosphoric acid from two bushels of bones. The dressing should be applied in two doses, half each time with an interval of two months between applications. The total cost would be 12*s.* 10*d.* per acre.

There were many large woods and plantations, especially of oak and ash. The Duke of Norfolk owned 1,500 acres of woodland near Sheffield, and other large estates throughout the county had extensive woods. There were also many new plantations, especially on hilltops, and trees were already being used to screen some of the ugliness of industrialization, as at Bowling Iron Works where trees were planted on spoil heaps.

On the country estates generation followed generation in the service of the landed gentry, and the children not so employed went to swell the growing population of the nearby towns. Farmers hired their workers at the annual statute hirings in the nearest market town, where eligible men and women stood waiting until their sturdy physique or sound experience induced some farmer to offer them employment for the year. To confirm the hiring the farmer gave his new servant a token coin. At harvest additional hands were hired from the gangs of Irish labourers who came over specially for the season.

Work on the land was hard and man had only the horse to help him with the heavier tasks of ploughing, harrowing and carting. The scythe for reaping and the flail for threshing were still widely used. Horse-gins were also in common use to provide power for such operations as corn-grinding: a horse plodding around and around turned a large horizontal wheel which was attached to the mill-stones.

Hedging, ditching and draining were carried out

7. Harewood House, the home of the Earl of Harewood, was built under the direction of Robert Adam of London and Carr of York and has a frontage of 284 feet. One hundred and fifty acres of pleasure grounds and gardens were laid out by 'Capability' Brown at a cost of £16,000.

after the crops had been harvested, and the labourer was the jack-of-all-trades, undertaking whatever work was required on the land or around the farm buildings. Large numbers of girls were employed in domestic service in both town and countryside. Like everyone else in the period they worked long hours, but the training which they received fitted them well for the duties of marriage and motherhood. They brought back to their homes good standards of domestic cleanliness and order. The educational value of such domestic service is often overlooked. In addition to keeping the large flagged farmhouse in spotless condition, preparing food for the household, scrubbing the clothes and 'minding' the children, the women of the farm helped with the milking and with cheese and butter making. They were to be found out of doors at haytime and harvest whenever another pair of hands was needed.

Butter, cheese and eggs were taken to the nearest town on market day, and selling them was the women's job. Cattle and corn were sold in special markets. Cows, sheep, pigs and geese were driven to market, often a journey of several miles. On market days town and countryside were brought close together in the interchange of trade and ideas. Schoolboys played truant to help the drovers (and surreptitiously milk the cows), drovers made advances to the town beauties, and the traders and farmers relaxed together in the numerous taverns.

The West Riding abounded with water-driven cornmills, but many windmills could also be seen on low eminences in the foothills of the Pennines and on the belt of magnesian limestone in the east. Air and water were still important sources of power, only gradually giving way to the more constant and reliable steam-engine.

# 2. Communications

The development of the West Riding woollen industry in the seventeenth century had been seriously hampered by poor communications. The long processions of pack horses, travelling by bridle-roads over hills and valleys, were inadequate to carry the growing volume of merchandise. The poor roads could not sustain a cart in bad weather, and even in summer were so rutted that travelling was slow and unreliable.

Rivers provided the surest means of conveyance and there was a great need to link the woollen area with the port of Kingston-upon-Hull. The Aire and Calder Navigation Act received the Royal Assent on 4 May 1699, thirty-eight years before any enactment for canal navigation in England. As soon as these rivers became navigable the whole of the woollen and surrounding areas were linked, via Leeds and Wakefield, with the port of Kingston-upon-Hull, bringing inestimable benefits to all. After the opening of the Duke of Bridgewater's canal in Lancashire, canals developed rapidly throughout the country, and many of these were in the West Riding. Canals were usually referred to as navigations and the labourers who constructed them were called navigators, later shortened to 'navvies'. In 1758 the navigation of the Calder was extended to Sowerby Bridge and was later linked to Manchester via Todmorden.

8. A packhorse bridge at Clayton West. For centuries a network of single-flagged roads formed the main link between the domestic weavers and their markets. These packhorse roads crossed the many streams by narrow bridges. Many, like this one, still survive.

The Barnsley Canal (Wakefield to Barnsley) was fifteen and one-eighth miles in length, and rose 117 feet by fifteen locks in the first two and three-quarter miles. Hiendley Reservoir was specially constructed to maintain the water level. It extended over 127 acres with a maximum depth of 40 feet. A powerful beam-engine lifted the water from the canal to the reservoir and in seasons of drought the water was re-admitted to the canal through a series of sluices. The canal had made possible the opening up of the Barnsley and

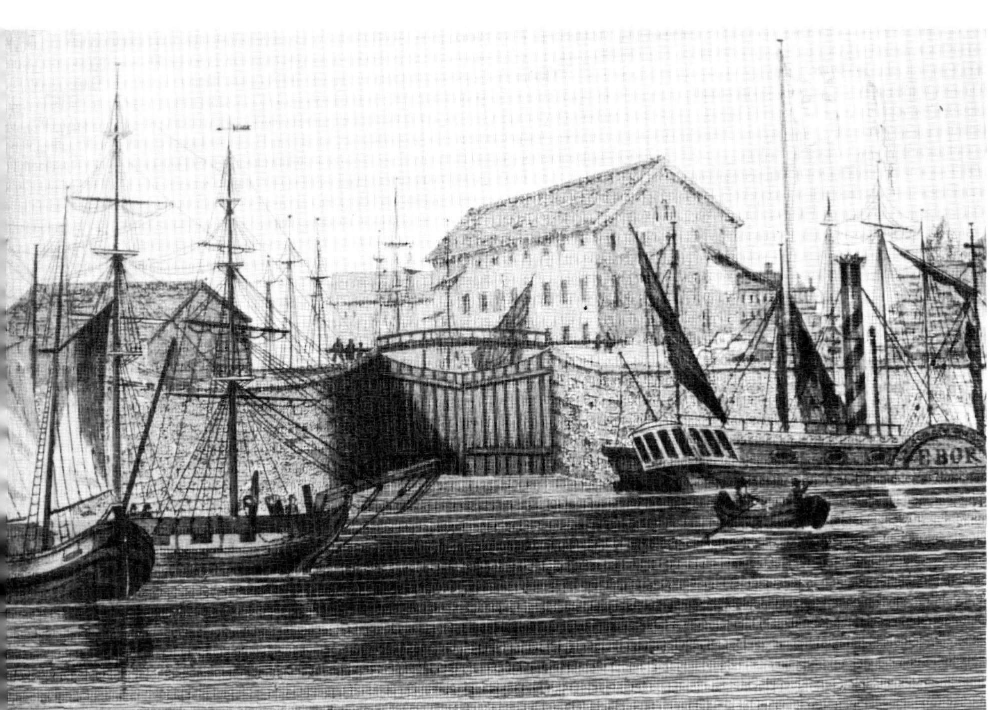


9. Goole Docks. Situated at the confluence of the Ouse and the Don, this inland port was constructed by the Aire and Calder Navigation Company. Paddle steamers were used for passenger transport.

Silkstone coalfields. Lime was brought from Knottingley to the Barnsley area, and this played an important part in converting the adjacent moorlands for agricultural use. This canal was spanned at Oakenshaw by a railway viaduct of three stone arches – the most substantial piece of stonework in the area. Mr Thornton, the contractor, had a wager with Mr Dyson, the engineer, that he would complete the work by a certain day, the loser to pay for a dinner for twelve guests from each side. The work proceeded well but, as the third arch neared completion, a misunderstanding arose between the English and Irish labourers, which resulted in a serious fight. The consequent delay in construction lost the wager for Mr Thornton, who, true to his promise, provided a sumptuous dinner at the new Normanton Hotel, which he had built to cater for the railway trade. After the various toasts, such songs as 'Steep, steep the goblet in the fount before us' were sung. When the party ended at 2.30 a.m. a special train took all the guests back to Wakefield. Mr Dyson was a generous man, and invited them to a repeat performance on 18 January 1842.

The Huddersfield Canal linked Sir John Ramsden's Canal to the Ashton-under-Lyne Canal, which made a through passage from the east to the west. The Huddersfield Canal rose 436 feet via forty-two locks to reach the summit level of 656 feet above sea-level, which was the highest in the kingdom. It then passed through Standedge by a tunnel 5,451 yards long and emerged into the Vale of Diggle in Saddleworth. The Marsden Tunnel, as it was called, was 9 feet wide, 17 feet high and contained 8 feet of water. There was no towing-path and the bargees pushed their boats through by 'legging' – lying on their backs and thrusting against the walls of the tunnel. It took one hour and twenty minutes to go through the tunnel. This east-to-west canal system was, by nine and three-quarter miles, the shortest of the four which crossed the country. It carried a heavy trade in corn, timber, woollen cloth, coals and raw materials for manufacture.

The Leeds to Liverpool Canal was $108\frac{3}{4}$ miles in length, 42 feet wide at the top, 27 feet at the bottom, and the water was 5 feet deep. Eleven years previously John

Priestley described it as 'one of the boldest and most magnificent projects hitherto attempted in Great Britain'. At Bingley Great Lock there were five rises in one range of gates and masonry. At its summit level it pierced the Pennines with a tunnel 1,640 yards long, and in the forty-one miles from Leeds Bridge to the Summit Lock at Greenberfield, it rose 411 feet 4 inches.

The Bradford Canal, three miles in length, joined the Leeds and Liverpool near Shipley, and was used by, among others, the proprietors of the Wibsey Low Moor and Bowling Iron Works. Flagstones and roofing slates for the London market and the east-coast towns passed along it, and transport for the woollen industry of the town was also provided.

The Thanet Canal, only one-third of a mile in length, was owned by the Earl of Thanet, and joined the Leeds and Liverpool near Skipton. It carried limestone from quarries a mile above Skipton Castle to the neighbourhood of Bradford, and for road-making beyond Leeds and Wakefield. The Sheffield Canal had only a short life before it faced the fierce competition of the railways.

During the late 1830s the stage-coach was at the height of its efficiency and popularity, and coaching provided employment, in one way or another, for thousands of people. The turnpike roads developed during the second half of the eighteenth century had provided the best road system the country had known since the withdrawal of the Romans. Roads spread out from London like the spokes of a wheel and, built according to the principles of road engineers such as Telford and Macadam, they were designed especially for coaches, which could travel at ten to twelve miles an hour without the hazards of broken axles caused by pot-holes, or sinking into the mud of an unsurfaced road. All the major communities in the West Riding were linked by such roads, some of them built by the remarkable Blind Jack Metcalfe of Knaresborough. Coaches left the principal towns daily on well-kept schedules.

10. Normanton Station: an important station at the junction of the North Midland Railway and the Leeds and Manchester Railway.

The turnpike roads and toll bridges were all private enterprises, sanctioned by Parliament, and much capital had gone into their construction. Then came

11. Stanley Ferry cast-iron aqueduct, built to carry the canal across the River Calder. This aqueduct, opened on 8 August 1839, was constructed by William Graham and Company, Milton Iron Works, near Sheffield. The trough is 165 feet in length and the total weight of the structure is 1,700 tons.

the railways, which offered greater speed in more comfort. Almost as soon as a railway was opened, the road traffic was severely reduced. Not everyone welcomed these changes. Richard Oastler, whom we shall meet later as the 'King of the Factory Children', wrote on 19 March:

I do not, I never did, I never shall like railroads. . . . I protest against the slavery entailed on passengers – the unsociableness of the whole concern – the breaking up of all connexion with intermediate towns and villages – the flying over the kingdom, and being no wiser, learning nothing of the country or its inhabitants. Formerly a journey was a lesson, a school, a lecture – we were always learning something everywhere, and a community of feeling, so necessary to the strength and safety of a nation, was fostered and established: now we arrive at the end of our journey as ignorant as when we started; we have formed no national sympathies, the two termini are England to us! I hate to be under the surveillance of the police attendants – the next step will be passports. I dislike the hurry, bustle, and danger – the hissing, grunting, roaring, whistling jargon of the engine is truly offensive. Then, the LOSS OF PROPERTY. Why, Sir, I verily believe, if an estimate were made of all the enormous losses to the creditors of the turnpike trusts and canals which have followed the introduction of railroads – the lowering of rents in towns and villages on the old roads, empty houses, diminished trade to shopkeepers, loss of employment to labourers, destruction of coaches, harness, and other matters consequent on the breaking up of the coaching, posting and carrying trades – I say, Sir, I believe all the property which has been thus destroyed (without one farthing's compensation) would, if calculated, prove to be as great in amount as all the money which the railroads have cost. All this loss has been incurred to pamper a few greedy men, to establish an unbearable monopoly, to make way for this new-fangled mode of binding England (lengthways and breadthways) in iron fetters!

Some coaches tried for a while to compete with the trains, one being the 'Old True Blue', which on 1 July was advertised 'to commence running from Leeds to Wakefield and Barnsley. The distance from Leeds to Barnsley will be performed in less time than by Rails and parcels conveyed on much less terms and without porterage'. The mail-coaches still ran and the Penny Post, introduced in 1840, had increased in popularity. There were still large areas of the West Riding not linked by railways, where the coaches provided regular services, as at Bradford where they linked the town with the railways at Leeds and Wakefield and also ran to Halifax, Skipton, Kendal, Lincoln – and to Ilkley during the season. Thirty carriers operated from the local inns, and provided a regular goods transport system to other West Riding towns.

The London coaches had now ceased to run. The famous 'Rockingham' had amalgamated with the 'Union' as 'Rockingham-Union', and the days when the London coaches stopped at Doncaster until the races were over were no more than a pleasant memory.

In spite of Oastler's criticisms, the railways expanded, and offered a transport service far superior to any yet known. It was now possible to travel by rail from Leeds to Kingston-upon-Hull; an extension of the North Midland linked York and Leeds with London; the short Sheffield-Rotherham Railway, built in 1838, joined the North Midland at Masborough.

The Manchester to Leeds Railway, along the Calder Valley, provided a link with Lancashire and a western outlet for commerce. This line, a great feat of engineering skill built under the supervision of George Stephenson, the railway genius of the age, was opened throughout its length on 1 March 1841, when the Directors and their friends made the journey in a special train decorated with banners, accompanied by bands and music. The *Leeds Mercury* hailed its opening as the greatest triumph of engineering science over natural obstacles of all railway projects in the kingdom:

The high chain of hills which separates Yorkshire from Lancashire, is only intersected by one valley, namely the Valley of the Calder, and that so narrow and winding, so full of natural irregularities, so lined with towns and villages, and so pre-occupied by the turnpike-road, the river and the canal, besides various bridle roads, as to make it exceedingly difficult to carry a railway through it. Yet by embankments and cuttings, by removing rocks and building up arches, by occasionally diverting the river and the road and often crossing both, by piercing the hills with short tunnels and taking first one side of the valley and then the other, a line has been constructed.

12. Selby Bridge, a timber bridge over the River Ouse. This bridge weighed seventy tons and worked on balls resembling 'cannon balls'. It could be opened and closed in one minute.

When the section of the line which passed Kirklees was built, the stone on Robin Hood's Grave was severely mutilated by the Irish navvies, who believed that a

13. Charleston Curves, Calder Valley. Road, railway, canal and river vie for space in the narrow valley. The railway engineers had intended to tunnel the hill, but the rock formation made this too difficult, so the line had to be taken around the hill in the valley, crossing road, river and canal where necessary.

chipping placed under a pillow was a cure for toothache.

Wherever railways and canals served the same areas competition arose, but the canals retained some of their trade. They were not so badly hit as the stage-coaches. On a single day it was possible to hear the call of the coaching horn, the hoot of the packet-boat and the whistle of the train – and to meet a herd of six or seven hundred cattle being driven southwards from Scotland to London.

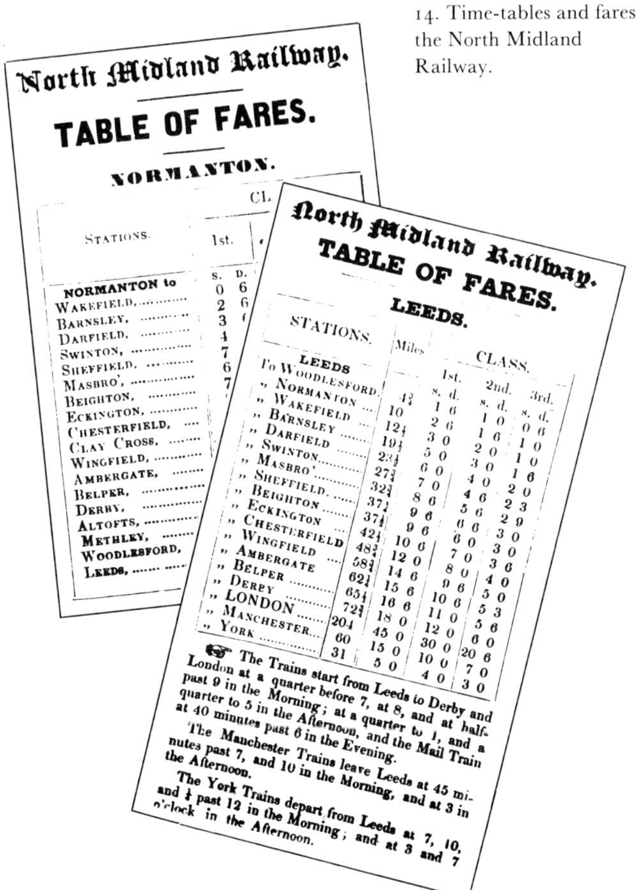

North Midland Railway.

TABLE OF FARES.

NORMANTON.

| STATIONS. | CL. 1st. s. | d. |
|---|---|---|
| NORMANTON to | | |
| WAKEFIELD, | 0 | 6 |
| BARNSLEY, | 2 | 6 |
| DARFIELD, | 3 | |
| SWINTON, | 4 | |
| SHEFFIELD, | 7 | |
| MASBRO', | 6 | |
| BEIGHTON, | 7 | |
| ECKINGTON, | | |
| CHESTERFIELD, | | |
| CLAY CROSS, | | |
| WINGFIELD, | | |
| AMBERGATE, | | |
| BELPER, | | |
| DERBY, | | |
| ALTOFTS, | | |
| METHLEY, | | |
| WOODLESFORD, | | |
| LEEDS, | | |

North Midland Railway.

TABLE OF FARES.

LEEDS.

| STATIONS. | Miles | CLASS. 1st. s. d. | 2nd. s. d. | 3rd. s. d. |
|---|---|---|---|---|
| LEEDS To WOODLESFORD. | 4¾ | 1 6 | 1 0 | 0 6 |
| ,, NORMANTON | 10 | 2 6 | 1 6 | 1 0 |
| ,, WAKEFIELD | 12¼ | 3 0 | 2 0 | 1 0 |
| ,, BARNSLEY | 19¼ | 5 0 | 3 0 | 1 6 |
| ,, DARFIELD | 23½ | 6 0 | 4 0 | 2 0 |
| ,, SWINTON | 27¾ | 7 0 | 4 6 | 2 3 |
| ,, MASBRO' | 32¾ | 8 6 | 5 6 | 2 9 |
| ,, SHEFFIELD | 37¼ | 9 6 | 6 6 | 3 0 |
| ,, BEIGHTON | 37½ | 9 6 | 6 0 | 3 0 |
| ,, ECKINGTON | 42¼ | 10 6 | 7 0 | 3 6 |
| ,, CHESTERFIELD | 48¾ | 12 0 | 8 0 | 4 0 |
| ,, WINGFIELD | 58¾ | 14 6 | 9 6 | 5 0 |
| ,, AMBERGATE | 62¼ | 15 6 | 10 6 | 5 3 |
| ,, BELPER | 65¼ | 16 6 | 11 0 | 5 6 |
| ,, DERBY | 72¾ | 18 0 | 12 0 | 6 0 |
| ,, LONDON | 204 | 45 0 | 30 0 | 20 6 |
| ,, MANCHESTER | 60 | 15 0 | 10 0 | 7 0 |
| ,, YORK | 31 | 5 0 | 4 0 | 3 0 |

☞ The Trains start from Leeds to Derby and London at a quarter before 7, at 8, and at half-past 9 in the Morning; at a quarter to 1, and a quarter to 5 in the Afternoon, and the Mail Train at 40 minutes past 6 in the Evening.

The Manchester Trains leave Leeds at 45 minutes past 7, and 10 in the Morning, and at 3 in the Afternoon.

The York Trains depart from Leeds at 7, 10, and ½ past 12 in the Morning; and at 3 and 7 o'clock in the Afternoon.

14. Time-tables and fares of the North Midland Railway.

15. The Waggoners' Inn, Northgate, Halifax. Three typical forms of transport, stage-coach, carrier's waggon and corn merchant's cart are seen in this picture. Waggons left Pickard's warehouse daily for all parts of the kingdom.

But more changes were on the way. The Sheffield to Manchester Railway had been sanctioned; on 16 September the *Sheffield Independent* reported that 500 able-bodied poor had volunteered to work on the Old Park contract, and 200 of them were already at work constructing the railway.

16. A simple method of mining coal. In 1842 a few pits were still worked by horse-gins, as pictured here.

# 3. Coal and iron

During 1842 coal was in great and growing demand and coal-mining had become a large and important industry. Steam-engines were generally used to operate the winding gear, and between Barnsley and Sheffield, where mines were being sunk deeper, much thought had been given to the kind and strength of rope required for this gear. At Day and Twibell's new colliery at Barnsley flat ropes six inches wide were used; the pulley wheels were very large and the shaft of 198 yards was well boarded with wooden conductors. At the foot of this shaft was a seam of coal ten feet thick which, despite the risk to the miners from 'firedamp' (a combustible gas), made the expense of sinking and working the pit a profitable one for the coal-masters. Besides debating the respective merits of round and flat ropes, mining engineers were striving to find better ways of ventilating the pits.

If mines were to go deeper and workings become more extensive, better ventilation was vital, not only to circulate fresh air and expel the noxious gases which pervaded the mines, but also to keep down the working temperature, which at Charlesworths' Dial Wood Colliery, near Midgley, with a shaft only eighty-five yards deep, was between 75 and 78°F at the banks. The normal system of ventilation was the hazardous one of circulating air by lighting a fire in the up-shaft, the hot air thus rising and drawing in fresh air through the down-shaft. About 1842 the first rotary machine used for the ventilation of mines in Yorkshire was installed at one of Earl Fitzwilliam's collieries at Elsecar – the invention of Benjamin Biram, the viewer of the colliery. The fan worked on the same principle as a water-wheel: placed at the foot of the up-shaft, it was driven by a jet of water striking upon small buckets fixed to its rim.

To control the flow of air underground, doors or 'gates' were erected in the passages. At the thin-seam pits these were usually pushed open by the corves (coal tubs) and closed by the draught of air after a corf had passed; but in the thick-seam pits where mine-passages were higher, children were employed as 'trappers' to open and shut the doors. This lonely and responsible task often fell to the youngest children, some of them only five or six years of age. Sometimes a kindly collier would give them a stump of candle. Little Sarah Gooder, aged eight years, a trapper at Gawber Pit, sometimes sang when she had a light, but not in the dark. 'I dare not sing then,' she said. Bad ventilation was often the fault of the miners, who failed to ensure that the doors were closed and who sometimes left them open deliberately because the draught made their candles burn higher and brighter.

Men, women and children all worked in the pits, usually in the most primitive conditions and always accompanied by dirt and danger. Colliers at the coal-face sometimes lay naked, hewing away at the coal in workings just high enough to crawl in; other men and boys, and occasionally women and girls, worked

17. The Middleton Colliery Coal Staith, Leeds. This mineral railway, using iron rails, ran $2\frac{1}{2}$ miles from the Middleton Colliery to the Coal Staith, Leeds. The two engines could draw 35 waggons of $3\frac{1}{2}$ tons each at two miles an hour. It was one of the earliest mineral railways in the world to use the steam locomotive. Very recently two men had been killed by the bursting of one of the boilers, so horses were then used, one horse drawing six waggons.

stripped to the waist. Water ran constantly from the water-bearing sandstones, or dripped down the shaft. This made life in the pits damp and dangerous. At Staincliffe Day Hole Pit, Mirfield, a Government official reported that he actually found men working in water and that the children's feet were never dry. The mine was the worst he had ever seen. There was no engine pump, only a hand pump which pumped the water into a sort of dam, from which it ran out again into the gates. He noted that 'this colliery, nevertheless, belongs to a gentleman reputed for his benevolence, but he knows nothing of his own pits'.

More than three-quarters of the children employed in the pits were 'hurriers' and they were usually engaged and paid by the miners. They helped the miner to load the coal into corves, then, harnessed to a corf, they

18. A miner's tally board, used for checking the tools issued to miners before reading was a universal skill.

dragged it to a pit shaft on all fours; this hard and crippling work commonly resulted in cases of spinal curvature. The harness consisted of a belt round the waist to which was attached a chain for linking with the corf. At Mr Ingham's pit at Thornhill, 247 children were employed, and 187 of these were hurriers. The youngest was a child aged six years and five months and the oldest just under eighteen years of age. Ann and Elizabeth Eggley worked as hurriers at Thorpe's Colliery, near Barnsley, and when Jellinger C. Symonds, an Assistant Commissioner of the Employment of Children in Mines Commission, visited this pit in the previous year he reported of them: 'Were they galley slaves their work could not be more oppressive and I believe not, in all probability, be so much'. Heartfelt words, for Symonds was no chair-bound official – he had tried to do the work himself! The two girls helped the miner to riddle the coal before loading, topped the corf with pieces of coal, which weighed up to one hundred pounds, then pushed the corf of 12½ cwt up an incline. Their twelve-hour working-day began between four and five o' clock each morning. Ann, who was sixteen years of age, received ten shillings a week for her labours – less than twopence an hour. She had worked in the pits since she was eleven, and wore trousers and big shoes, which were clinkered and nailed. Neither she nor her sister had ever been to school. At home they shared a small two-roomed house with eight other members of the family, and at night they were often too tired to wash, and fell asleep after their one good meal of the day.

In the larger pits, like the Upper and Lower Elsecar mines belonging to Earl Fitzwilliam, horses were used to draw the corves through the long main gates, and boys aged between eleven and fourteen were employed as horse-drivers. In pits where there was a very steep incline, 'Jenny boys', aged between eleven and sixteen, operated a chain-and-pulley arrangement which controlled the speed of the corves along the gradient. In the thick-seam pits the working-day was of ten or eleven hours duration; it was a little less in the thin-seam pits, where working conditions were harder. The day commenced before five o' clock in the morning and the average pay of the adult miner was about fifteen shillings a week, often paid fortnightly, sometimes at a local inn, where the miner was expected to pay his debts – and often spent more before going home. Before setting out for work his normal meal was bread or oatcake and milk or porridge. He took chunks of bread with pieces of cheese, bacon or 'fat' to eat in the pit, and on his return home he had a hot meal of meat, vegetables and Yorkshire pudding. Some miners kept a pig and many grew their own vegetables; others indulged in poaching, so that from time to time rabbits and game provided a feast for their families.

Accidents in pits were frequent, but except in the case of a major disaster they passed almost without notice. 'Firedamp' was the cause of many explosions, attributable sometimes to the carelessness of the miners, who in spite of the introduction of the Davy lamp, to reduce the danger of gas explosion, preferred the light of an open candle. Where these lamps were supplied, men had been known to take off the top and even make a hole in the gauze to allow more light to pass. The year 1842 began with an explosion at Hopwood's Pit, Barnsley, which killed a man named Soldier Billy, together with two girls named Mallinder and a girl named Day. A report of the accident said: 'What makes this melancholy case more distressing, the mother, a widow, was solely dependent on the earnings of her two children, the Mallinders.' Such was the real cost of winning the nation's coal.

Disputes between miners and coal-masters were frequent, and occasionally the masters met the demands of their workers, as at Traviss and Horsfall's Colliery at Worsbrough, where the men ended their dispute and returned to work in June. A significant note in the report of this event was that 'four of the turn-out colliers have gone to London to be examined before Mr Ferrand's Committee' (an official investigation into mining conditions).

Strong and individualistic, yet with the group loyalty of a Scottish clansman, the miner could be distinguished by the blue scars on his face and hands, where open cuts had filled with coal-dust before healing. Dust took its toll of lungs, too, and long hours without sunlight, difficult working conditions, the lack of holidays – two days at Christmas were the only regular holidays – and the pressures of an overcrowded home made him an old man at fifty. Although the miners suffered so severely, it was upon their labours that the industrial might of England was built, for coal provided the power of the steam-engine, heat to smelt iron and steel to make machines.

However, there was hope of better days to come. Men of goodwill, including some coal-masters, were concerned about improving working conditions. Earl Fitzwilliam and his agent had already provided their workers with reasonable homes at a nominal rent, gifts of food at certain times of the year, sick-pay and a small pension for those who became permanently disabled.

19. The Southwark Iron Bridge, built by Walkers of the Holmes Works, Rotherham, and weighing between 5,000 and 6,000 tons. Opened in 1819, this toll-bridge cost about £287,000. Walkers were reputed to be the only firm in the country capable of making an iron bridge of this size.

More important, the miners were beginning to organize themselves, and in November 1842 a meeting was held at Wakefield which led to the establishment of the Miners' Philanthropic Society. The appointment of a paid secretary made it possible, for the first time, for someone to speak for the miners without running the risk of victimization.

Ironstone mining and smelting had become important industries, notably at Wibsey Low Moor, Bowling,

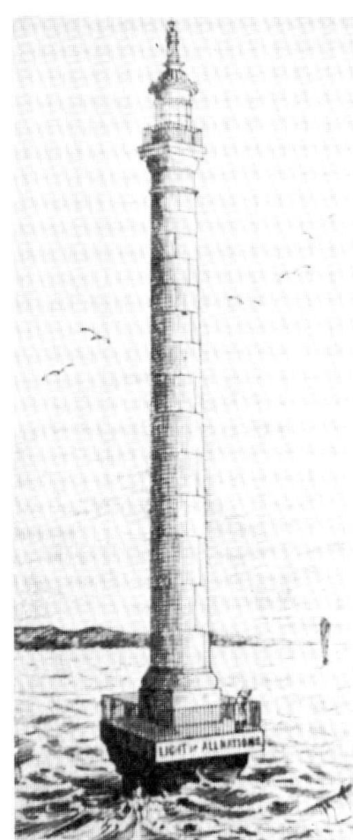

20. The lighthouse that never was! In 1841 Newton Chambers of Chapeltown, Sheffield, supplied castings for a lighthouse to be built on the Goodwin Sands, to the design of Mr William Bush, civil engineer. It was to consist of hollow castings, placed one above the other and bolted together. The work was abandoned by Trinity House when the base was unseated during a thunderstorm.

and around Sheffield and Rotherham. Messrs Graham's ironstone mine at Tankersley had a shaft fifty yards deep, whilst, at Thorncliffe, Newton and Chambers had a day hole pit from which they worked a seam nine feet thick from a single semicircular face. In 1842 the Low Moor Ironworks, which had been in constant use since 1789, employed 1,200 persons.

A traveller journeying to Sheffield from Leeds would be met with a scene perhaps even more startling than that which greeted Cobbett twelve years earlier. A shrewd and careful observer, he wrote:

> All the way along from Leeds to Sheffield it is coal and iron, and iron and coal. It was dark before we reached Sheffield; so that we saw the iron furnaces in all the horrible splendour of their everlasting blaze. Nothing can be conceived more grand or more terrific than the yellow waves of fire that incessantly issue from the top of these furnaces, some of which are close by the way-side. Nature has placed the beds of iron and the beds of coal alongside of each other, and art has taught man to make one to operate upon the other, as to turn the iron-stone into liquid matter, which is drained off from the bottom of the furnace, and afterwards moulded into blocks and bars, and all sorts of things. The combustibles are put into the top of the furnace, which stands thirty, forty or fifty feet up in the air, and the ever-blazing mouth of which is kept supplied with coal and coke and ironstone from little iron waggons forced up by steam, and brought down again to be refilled. It is a surprising thing to behold; and it is impossible to behold it without being convinced that, whatever other nations may do with cotton and with wool, they will never equal England with regard to things made of iron and steel.

In 1842 there was a severe trade depression in Sheffield and it was said that manufacturers could neither afford to close the factories nor profitably keep them open. In 1839 Americans owed them £600,000 which they were unable to recover. In spite of the depression the Sheffield manufacturers were still optimistic about the future and new firms continued to come into existence, including the firm of Thomas Firth and Sons which was established in 1842. At that time there were ninety-seven furnaces in Sheffield and 774 melting holes. Its manufacturers produced stove-grates, fenders and fire-irons, anvils and vices, steel taps, axles and coach-springs, scissors, razors, guns and powder-flasks, magnets, nails, needles, fish-hooks, scythes, sickles, snuffers, nippers, nutcrackers, steam-engines, boilers, wire, weighing-machines, lancets and phlemes (bleeding boxes – see Chapter 7), and a vast range of cutlery and tools. In 1840 the first successful experiment in electro-plating had taken place, but the old-established Sheffield plate still reigned supreme.

Rotherham was famous for the manufacture of stove-grates and the rolling of bar, rod and sheet steel for Sheffield consumption and for markets overseas. A fresh impetus was given to the iron and steel industries by the requirements of the new railways. Other branches of the industry were expanding; Messrs Stubbs of Warrington, edge-tool manufacturers, found that their Masborough premises were too small and in 1842 erected new buildings at the Holmes, at a cost of £20,000. Although not yet brought into industrial use, Nasmyth's steam hammer had just been invented, and Rotherham's future as a great iron and steel centre seemed assured.

# 4. Textiles and other industries

21. The Crank Mill, Morley, built by the Earl of Dartmouth in 1790, was the first steam-powered mill to be built in Morley.

The 'King of the Factory Children' was Richard Oastler, who fought unceasingly for the betterment of their conditions. Imprisoned in the Fleet Prison for debt, he continued the fight by publication of the *Fleet Papers* from his cell, where he was visited by an endless procession of sympathizers and informants. The heading of each paper set forth his creed: The altar, the throne and the cottage – Property has its duties, as well as its rights – The husbandman that laboureth, must be first partaker of the fruits – He shall judge the poor of the people, He shall save the children of the needy, and shall break in pieces the oppressor.

His general attack was upon the factory system: his immediate aims were to find means of reducing the poverty of the mill-workers, to ensure full employment, and, above all, to secure a reduction in their long hours, and improve the working conditions of the children.

In the issue of the *Fleet Papers* dated 9 April 1842, he quoted from the journal of his friend, Mark Crabtree, who had just returned from the West Riding of Yorkshire:

As I was going from Bradford to Huddersfield one morning, between five and six o' clock, in the middle of January last, the roads being then ancle deep in snow, and which was also coming down in large flakes, I met numbers of females going to the factories, and scarcely a male to be seen. A married woman said to her companion as I passed, 'My poor bairn DID cry this morning when I left it!' I asked her how old her baby was? and she said, 'FIVE WEEKS, SIR!' I then asked her where her husband was? She answered, 'He is in bed, Sir; he has nothing to do.' A gentleman on horseback was passing, and heard our conversation; he remarked, 'This is a most horrible system – it is entirely destroying the morals of the people of these districts.' I saw a poor man with two little girls, nine and twelve years old – one had hold of each hand. I asked him, 'Where are you going?' 'To seek work for these children!' was his answer. He added, 'It is hard work, master, to be thrown out of work, and to be forced to turn these poor things into the factories! I was a spinner, but my spinning frame was double-decked [joined to another], so

22. The Piece Hall, Halifax. Halls such as this were erected in the principal woollen towns as markets for manufacturers, many of whom were initially self-employed. This piece hall was built in 1779 by the shalloon, worsted and woollen manufacturers of the town, and contained 315 rooms.

ONE man now works them both, and I cannot get a job anywhere; so I must be idle, and these children must earn MY bread! It is hard work, Sir!' And then the poor fellow wept. The above are a few of the many hundred cases which might be mentioned in reference to females employed in factories.

Crabtree also recorded a conversation he had with a woman comber when he visited a public house. She began work at six in the morning. For breakfast she was allowed a fifteen-minute break, for lunch one hour, for tea fifteen minutes, and her working day ended at 7.30 in the evening. Four times a minute she lifted above her head a comb which weighed twenty-four pounds – a total of ninety-six pounds every minute throughout the working week. When she finished her work she was unable to eat and resorted to the public house because 'We must have something – I brought this bread and butter with me this morning and you see I have not eaten it'. Small wonder that her appearance was very much emaciated and that Crabtree considered she was hastening to an early grave.

On 16 April, Oastler's pen was directed against the system which had driven men out of the mills and employed the cheaper labour of young children in their stead, so that men were forced to live on the earnings of their infants and wives. John Fielden, MP, a manufacturer and friend of Oastler, supported the campaign. He had himself confirmed that a child walked up to twenty-five miles a day in following a spinning-machine, which, added to the journey to and from home, could total thirty miles a day. Indeed some children were so tired at the end of the day that they tried to sleep in the mill, near the boiler, and had to be turned out and whipped all the way home.

Some idea of the extent of the Yorkshire worsted trade may be obtained from a survey made by Factory Inspectors four years previously. There were then 347 mills, nearly all employed in making pure worsteds, with machines producing a total of 5,781 horse-power. They were driven by either water or steam, or a combination of the two; 26,581 people were employed, the equivalent of five sixths of the total persons employed in the worsted trade in the whole of England. In the whole of the country there were 4,651 children aged between nine and thirteen working in worsted mills, and of these 4,185 were in the West Riding of Yorkshire. Of those aged between thirteen and eighteen, 11,951 out of a total of 14,023 worked in the West Riding. Nearly two-thirds of the total work-force consisted of children and young people aged eighteen or under.

The value of worsted yarn exports for 1842 was £637,305, most of it from the West Riding, and in the same year 1,979,492 pieces of woollen and worsted stuffs were exported. These exports represented a world-wide trade, and returns showed a decline in trade with the East Indies and China, and a great increase in sales to the Continent. Germany was the best customer, buying 620,044 pieces, the USA next with 285,053 pieces, and Holland third with 189,851 pieces. Worsted goods bore such names as princettas, lastings, grosgrains, camblets, wildbores or bambazets, and shalloons; the last, a cloth thirty to thirty four inches wide, cost 18*s.* to 56*s.* per piece of 28 yards.

Expanding output and extensive markets did not, however, prevent unemployment. A report from Dewsbury, the centre of the blanket trade, in the *Wakefield Journal* of 13 May, said:

> The great demon of mechanism smokes and thunders as much as ever, and conjures, in no time, incalculable quantities of should-be manufactures, almost independently of manual exertion. The formerly industrious operatives, unemployed, friendless and unpitied, while killing time, by sauntering about the marketplace, behold with indignation, the waggons of steam-made goods, which daily pass before them.

In the previous month a woman travelled to Sheepridge from above Golcar, where she lived, twenty times (260 miles) without obtaining a single warp to weave.

23. Halifax woollen mills.

Machinery was not protected, so there were many accidents. On 2 June an accident was reported from Aldam's Mill, Dewsbury:

> Yesterday, 2nd, a poor orphan child by the name of Thomas Jolly, had his thigh broke and other severe bruises, by playing with a strap that was turning a wheel. He was caught by it and was supposed to have gone round the wheel not less than five hundred times before he was extricated. But little hopes are entertained of his recovery.

In the title of a Directory published by William White in 1842, the woollen district is defined as follows: 'Leeds, Bradford, Halifax, Huddersfield, Wakefield,

24. The interior of Marshall's Flax Mill, Holbeck, Leeds, which was opened in 1840 with a Temperance Tea for the firm's 2,600 workers. In December 1842 the Council of the Institution of Civil Engineers awarded a Premium of books to J. Combe for his description and drawings of this mill.

Dewsbury, Heckmondwike, Bingley, Keighley, and about six hundred villages and hamlets, and eight hundred thousand inhabitants.' Each of these centres specialized in one or more branches of the industry.

An important development had been the introduction of 'shoddy', a material made by a mixture of sheep-wool and rag-wool, the proportion of each determining the quality of the cloth. It was thought to have been first produced by Benjamin Law in 1813, but several others began running rag machines about the same time. Batley, which had long been engaged in woollen manufacture, became the centre of the shoddy trade, which spread outwards to the neighbouring towns and villages. Some rags for the making of shoddy were imported from the Continent, and a halfpenny a pound duty was charged on them. This mixture of rag-wool with the cheaper kinds of unused wool made possible the production of good cheap clothing for all classes of society, and this was of particular value to the working class. Nothing was wasted, and the shoddy manufacturers claimed: 'If it has two ends we can spin it'. Even the dust from the mill floor was swept up and sold as a fertilizer.

Mungo, a fine ground cloth, developed from the shoddy trade about 1834. Mungo cloth was made from pieces of old garments and clippings of new cloth from the tailors' shops. Its unusual name is said to have arisen from the reply given by one of the early manufacturers when doubts were expressed about the likelihood of it selling. His Yorkshire reply was, 'It mun go'.

Flax-spinning was carried on at Leeds, where it had been introduced in 1788. The principal manufacturer was John Marshall, who was stigmatized by Oastler as a monopolist:

It is well known in Leeds, that Mr Marshall would formerly contrive (when a man with small capital embarked more than his all in a flax-mill, and the poor fellow was hoping to obtain a fair reward for his outlay and industry) to lower the prices of yarn, to the certain ruin of the beginner, and afterwards, when the novice was ruined, Mr M. advanced

25. A view of the Leeds industries from Rope Hill, *c.*1840.

the prices, thus regaining all that he had lost, when the man of small capital was gone! There never was a more thorough MONOPOLIST, in this world, than Mr John Marshall, the flax-spinner, of Leeds.

Marshall sent most of his flax yarn to Ireland to be made into linen, but some of the coarser yarns were sent to Barnsley, where the industry was based mainly on sheetings and towels.

Cotton-mills existed in several places, including Todmorden and Keighley, and there were silk-mills at Leeds, Halifax, Huddersfield and Hebden Bridge.

Pottery of all kinds was made in the West Riding. In June one of the best-known potteries closed down and the premises were advertised:

To be let, and entered upon immediately, all those extensive China and Earthenware Works in Swinton, near Rotherham, called The Rockingham Works, late in the occupation of Messrs Brameld. . . . N.B. A very large assortment of China

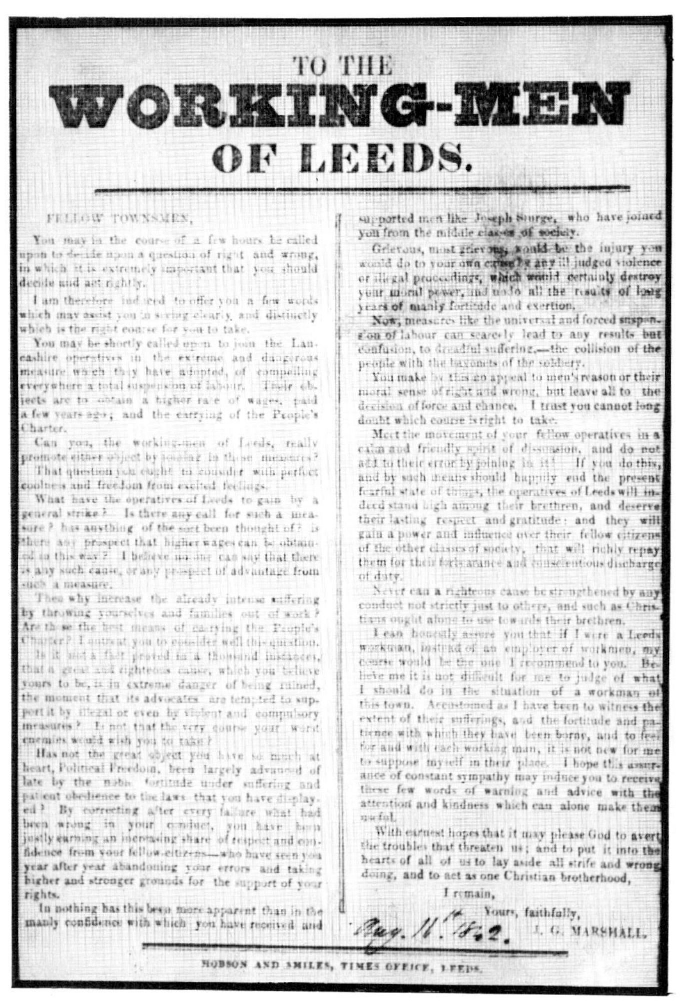

TO THE

# WORKING-MEN OF LEEDS.

FELLOW TOWNSMEN,

You may in the course of a few hours be called upon to decide upon a question of right and wrong, in which it is extremely important that you should decide and act rightly.

I am therefore induced to offer you a few words which may assist you in seeing clearly and distinctly which is the right course for you to take.

You may be shortly called upon to join the Lancashire operatives in the extreme and dangerous measure which they have adopted, of compelling everywhere a total suspension of labour. Their objects are to obtain a higher rate of wages, paid a few years ago; and the carrying of the People's Charter.

Can you, the working-men of Leeds, really promote either object by joining in these measures?

That question you ought to consider with perfect coolness and freedom from excited feelings.

What have the operatives of Leeds to gain by a general strike? Is there any call for such a measure? has anything of the sort been thought of? is there any prospect that higher wages can be obtained in this way? I believe no one can say that there is any such cause, or any prospect of advantage from such a measure.

Then why increase the already intense suffering by throwing yourselves and families out of work? Are these the best means of carrying the People's Charter? I entreat you to consider well this question.

Is it not a fact proved in a thousand instances, that a great and righteous cause, which you believe yours to be, is in extreme danger of being ruined, the moment that its advocates are tempted to support it by illegal or even by violent and compulsory measures? Is not that the very course your worst enemies would wish you to take?

Has not the great object you have so much at heart, Political Freedom, been largely advanced of late by the noble fortitude under suffering and patient obedience to the laws that you have displayed? By correcting after every failure what had been wrong in your conduct, you have been justly earning an increasing share of respect and confidence from your fellow-citizens—who have seen you year after year abandoning your errors and taking higher and stronger grounds for the support of your rights.

In nothing has this been more apparent than in the manly confidence with which you have received and supported men like Joseph Sturge, who have joined you from the middle classes of society.

Grievous, most grievous, would be the injury you would do to your own cause by any ill judged violence or illegal proceedings, which would certainly destroy your moral power, and undo all the results of long years of manly fortitude and exertion.

Now, measures like the universal and forced suspension of labour can scarcely lead to any results but confusion, to dreadful suffering,—the collision of the people with the bayonets of the soldiery.

You make by this no appeal to men's reason or their moral sense of right and wrong, but leave all to the decision of force and chance. I trust you cannot long doubt which course is right to take.

Meet the movement of your fellow operatives in a calm and friendly spirit of dissuasion, and do not add to their error by joining in it! If you do this, and by such means should happily end the present fearful state of things, the operatives of Leeds will indeed stand high among their brethren, and deserve their lasting respect and gratitude; and they will gain a power and influence over their fellow citizens of the other classes of society, that will richly repay them for their forbearance and conscientious discharge of duty.

Never can a righteous cause be strengthened by any conduct not strictly just to others, and such as Christians ought alone to use towards their brethren.

I can honestly assure you that if I were a Leeds workman, instead of an employer of workmen, my course would be the one I recommend to you. Believe me it is not difficult for me to judge of what I should do in the situation of a workman of this town. Accustomed as I have been to witness the extent of their sufferings, and the fortitude and patience with which they have been borne, and to feel for and with each working man, it is not new for me to suppose myself in their place. I hope this assurance of constant sympathy may induce you to receive these few words of warning and advice with the attention and kindness which can alone make them useful.

With earnest hopes that it may please God to avert the troubles that threaten us; and to put it into the hearts of all of us to lay aside all strife and wrong doing, and to act as one Christian brotherhood,

I remain,

Yours, faithfully,

Aug. 11th 1842. J. G. MARSHALL.

HOBSON AND SMILES, TIMES OFFICE, LEEDS.

26. Marshall's letter to his workpeople during the period of unrest in 1842.

and Earthenware is now selling off at the Works at very Reduced Prices.

The considerable and varied engineering industry made a notable contribution to progress, and engineers such as Peter Fairbairn of Leeds, who invented and improved machines for the flax industry, were in the forefront of this advance. Wire was also being finely drawn: one firm at Halifax wove this into blinds and mosquito nets.

Probably the most ancient industry in the county was lead-mining, which was scattered over an area of a thousand square miles of Yorkshire, mainly in the Dales. In 1838 the output of the mines around Greenhow Hill, three miles WSW of Pateley Bridge, amounted to 2,000 tons.

The wide range of industries included brass, soap and chemicals, and glass. Two of the more important glassworks were those of John and Joshua Bower at Leeds, but there were others in various parts of the West Riding. At Ossett Street-side, a notable improvement was made in 1837 by Richard Baker and Son, which enabled them to make glass so pliable that it could be woven into cloth of the finest texture. In January 1838 they had presented to the Queen an elegant glass apron, having the appearance of silk, and feeling quite as soft to the touch.

Every trade and craft developed its own occupational names, and in this respect the woollen industry claimed pride of place with such names as teazers, hand-raisers, slubbers, willeyers, higglers, burlers, carders, scribblers, croppers, piecers, pluckers, warpers, fullers, tenterers, drawers and pick-locks.

# 5. Government and politics

27. Lord Wharncliffe, Lord Lieutenant of the West Riding of Yorkshire in 1842.

The Lord Lieutenant, the Rt. Hon. James Archibald Stuart Wortley Mackenzie, Lord Wharncliffe, represented the Queen in the West Riding of Yorkshire in 1842. He recommended those to be appointed magistrates, raised the militia and acted as the focal point of county government. The 238 magistrates for the West Riding, drawn almost exclusively from the ranks of the gentry and clergy, supervised the activities of various officials and dealt with petty crime in their own localities. When they met in Quarter Sessions their administrative jurisdiction covered the county, and they dealt also with the more serious criminal offences, except those reserved for the County Assizes at York. In times of civil disturbance the aid of the military forces could be invoked, and it was a magistrate who read the Riot Act and called upon the soldiers to maintain or restore order.

At the spring Quarter Sessions on 4 April 1842 the magistrates ordered, among other things, that £700 be granted for enlarging the chapel of the West Riding Pauper Lunatic Asylum at Wakefield and that the boundary wall of the additional buildings at the House of Correction be proceeded with forthwith; that the piers and abutments of Tadcaster Bridge be repaired and that ashlar be replaced with gritstone; that £53. 13*s*. be allowed for making an additional bedroom

**MIDSUMMER ESTREAT, 1841.**

| Cawood, Wistow, and Doncaster Soke, exempt from payment of No. 2. Ripon Liberty, exempt from payment of Nos. 3 and 4. Ainsty exempt from payment of No. 5. | Annual Value of the Riding. | 1. For the Governor, Chaplain and other Officers of York Castle, half a year's Salary, maintaining Prisoners therein, and supporting Judge's Lodgings, £1300. For Repairs and Bills at the Register Office, £257 5s. | | | 2. For Repairs of Riding Bridges and Roads over the same, £2206. Bridge Surveyor's half a year's Salary, £350. | | | 3. For the Public Stock £2600. Apprehending and Prosecuting Felons and Misdemeanants, £1400. Conveyance of Prisoners to York and Wakefield, and to and from the different Sessions, £1100. Coroners' Inquisitions, and expences relating thereto, £1300. High Constables' half a year's Salary, £900. | | | 4. For the Keeper, Chaplain, and other Officers of the House of Correction, half a year's Salary, Maintaining and Clothing the Prisoners therein, £3700. Repairs at the House of Correction, £300. For providing additional accommodation for Prisoners in the House of Correction, £1395 13s. 11d. Repairs at Clerk of the Peace's Office, £58 16s. 10d. Repairs of Court Houses, £300. Repairs and furnishing at the Pauper Lunatic Asylum, £450. For New Buildings at ditto, £1500. | | | 5. For preparing and printing the Register of Voters, £707 9s. 8d. | | | For Repairs of Bridges in the Wapentake of Agbrigg and Morley, £91 6s. 8d. Ditto in Claro, £91 12s. 9d. Ditto in Staincliffe and Ewcross, £100. Ditto in Strafforth and Tickhill, £78 9s. 2d. | | | TOTAL. | | |
|---|---|---|---|---|---|---|---|---|---|---|---|---|---|---|---|---|---|---|---|---|---|---|
| | £. | £. | s. | d. | £. | s. | d. | £. | s. | d. | £. | s. | d. | £. | s. | d. | £. | s. | d. | £. | s. | d. |
| **WAPONTAKES, &c.** | 1,983,966 | 1,557 | 5 | 0 | 2,556 | 0 | 0 | 10,300 | 0 | 0 | 7,704 | 10 | 9 | 707 | 9 | 8 | 361 | 8 | 7 | 23,186 | 14 | 0 |
| Agbrigg and Morley, (except such part thereof as is within the Borough of Leeds, viz:—£53,104.) ........ | 658,744 | 517 | 1 | 3 | 856 | 1 | 0 | 3,506 | 3 | 8 | 2,622 | 13 | 5 | 242 | 3 | 4 | 91 | 6 | 8 | 7,835 | 9 | 4 |
| Ainsty, ........................ | 59,478 | 46 | 13 | 9 | 77 | 5 | 10 | 316 | 11 | 6 | 236 | 16 | 0 | | | | | | | 677 | 7 | 1 |
| Barkston-Ash, Cawood, and Wistow, £86,381. | 80,330 | 63 | 1 | 1 | 104 | 7 | 9 | 427 | 11 | 2 | 319 | 16 | 5 | 29 | 10 | 8 | | | | 944 | 7 | 1 |
| | 6,051 | 4 | 15 | 0 | | | | 32 | 4 | 1 | 24 | 1 | 10 | 2 | 4 | 6 | | | | 63 | 5 | 5 |
| Claro, ........ £196,226. | 147,432 | 115 | 14 | 6 | 191 | 11 | 10 | 784 | 14 | 2 | 586 | 19 | 6 | 54 | 4 | 0 | 68 | 17 | 1 | 1,802 | 1 | 1 |
| Ripon Liberty, | 48,794 | 38 | 6 | 0 | 63 | 8 | 2 | | | | | | | 17 | 18 | 9 | 22 | 15 | 8 | 142 | 8 | 7 |
| Osgoldcross, (except the Township of Pontefract, viz:—£9,820.)...... | 107,888 | 84 | 13 | 8 | 140 | 4 | 1 | 574 | 4 | 9 | 429 | 10 | 9 | 39 | 13 | 3 | | | | 1,268 | 6 | 6 |
| Skyrack, (except such part thereof as is within the Borough of Leeds, viz:—£212,798.) ................ | 109,473 | 85 | 18 | 7 | 142 | 5 | 3 | 582 | 13 | 5 | 435 | 16 | 11 | 40 | 4 | 11 | | | | 1,286 | 19 | 1 |
| Staincliffe and Ewcross, ............ | 256,556 | 201 | 7 | 6 | 333 | 8 | 0 | 1,365 | 10 | 6 | 1,021 | 8 | 7 | 94 | 6 | 4 | 100 | 0 | 0 | 3,116 | 0 | 11 |
| Staincross, ........................ | 93,725 | 73 | 11 | 4 | 121 | 15 | 11 | 498 | 17 | 1 | 373 | 3 | 0 | 34 | 9 | 1 | | | | 1,101 | 16 | 5 |
| Strafforth and Tickhill, Doncaster Soke, (except the Township of Doncaster, viz:—27,813.).. £415,495. | 404,464 | 317 | 9 | 2 | 525 | 12 | 2 | 2,152 | 15 | 5 | 1,610 | 6 | 0 | 148 | 13 | 9 | 78 | 9 | 2 | 4,833 | 5 | 8 |
| | 11,031 | 8 | 13 | 2 | | | | 58 | 14 | 3 | 43 | 18 | 4 | 4 | 1 | 1 | | | | 115 | 6 | 10 |
| **TOTAL,** ........................ | 1,983,966 | 1,557 | 5 | 0 | 2,556 | 0 | 0 | 10,300 | 0 | 0 | 7,704 | 10 | 9 | 707 | 9 | 8 | 361 | 8 | 7 | 23,186 | 14 | 0 |

28. The West Riding Magistrates' Estreat for Midsummer 1841, published in 1842.

for the keeper of the Knaresborough Court House.

They agreed that a memorial be presented to the Queen in Council, praying for the grant of an additional Gaol Delivery for the County of York, in the long interval between the midsummer Assizes and the spring Assizes. In the memorial it was claimed that at the commencement of the late spring Assizes there were in the gaol at York Castle 162 prisoners for offences committed within the county, 2 for offences in the city of York, besides 10 out on bail. Of this number 7 had been committed in the previous July, 12 in August, 9 in September and 31 in October, and that this was too long a period of imprisonment before trial. In addition, because of the large numbers of prisoners, the Assizes lasted for nineteen days, even though it had the assistance of a third judge, the consequence of which was an additional expense averaging £18 for each prosecution and great inconvenience to all the parties involved, as well as a degree of insecurity in the parishes because so many constables were away from their posts. All this fell particularly heavily on the West Riding as 162 of the 174 prisoners came from this division.

Criminal cases were often dealt with harshly. At the January West Riding Quarter Sessions, John Carless was found guilty of burglariously entering the parish church at Mirfield and was sentenced to transportation for life. Seven other men received sentences of transportation for seven years. Their offences involved theft of various items – fowls at Halifax, a leather skin at Rothwell, wearing apparel at Huddersfield, boots at Bradford, brushes at Huddersfield, lead at Halifax, and money at Bradford, respectively.

A number of courts exercised civil jurisdiction in various forms, and their verdicts were not always given on the basis of logic and reason. On 20 January the case of Sidebottom *v.* Davies was heard before the Sheriff's Court. The jury was locked away for five hours and then brought in a verdict for the plaintiff. One juror jocularly remarked that they had been deliberating for five hours and then drawn cuts for the verdict after all. The defendant's solicitors immediately called for the learned assessor to discharge the jury and demanded another trial, which was granted. The jury were lucky to escape with a severe reprimand.

The Report of the Visiting Justices of the West Riding House of Correction at Wakefield for 1842 showed that 4,430 persons had been committed to the prison during the last year, the greatest number in custody at any one time being 955. Discipline was good except among the juvenile offenders, and the chaplain was directed to pay special attention to them. They were taught reading, writing and arithmetic for three hours every day. The success of a new diet introduced in the previous August gave the justices most satisfaction. It was claimed that it had reduced the number of sick prisoners from $4\frac{1}{5}$ per cent to $3\frac{1}{3}$ per cent. The prison expenses for the year were £11,434. 12*s*. 7*d*., and the prisoners were employed in the usual prison trades, to which a new trade of mat-making had been added. The following is an extract from the report:

| *Trade* | *No. Employed* | *Total Earnings* | *Individual Earnings* |
|---|---|---|---|
| Wool dressing | 402 | £701 16*s*. 10*d*. | £1 14*s*. 11*d*. |
| Wool combing | $19\frac{1}{2}$ | £183 15*s*. $0\frac{1}{2}$*d*. | £9 8*s*. 6*d*. |
| Shoe making | $8\frac{1}{2}$ | £99 19*s*. 7*d*. | £11 15*s*. 3*d*. |
| Mat making | $21\frac{1}{2}$ | £52 5*s*. $0\frac{1}{4}$*d*. | £2 8*s*. 8*d*. |
| Sundry employment | 37 | £32 4*s*. $7\frac{1}{2}$*d*. | 17*s*. 5*d*. |
| | 488·50 | £1070 1*s*. $1\frac{1}{4}$*d*. | Average earnings of each prisoner: £2 3*s*. 10*d*. |

29. The West Riding Court House, Wakefield.

The average cost to keep each prisoner was £14. 10*s*. 3*d*., being a decrease of £1. 8*s*. 9*d*. on the last year's cost.

On 3 May the second National Petition for the People's Charter was presented in the House of Commons by Thomas Duncombe, MP for Finsbury. Thomas Babington Macaulay spoke brilliantly in opposing it and the petition was rejected. Feelings ran

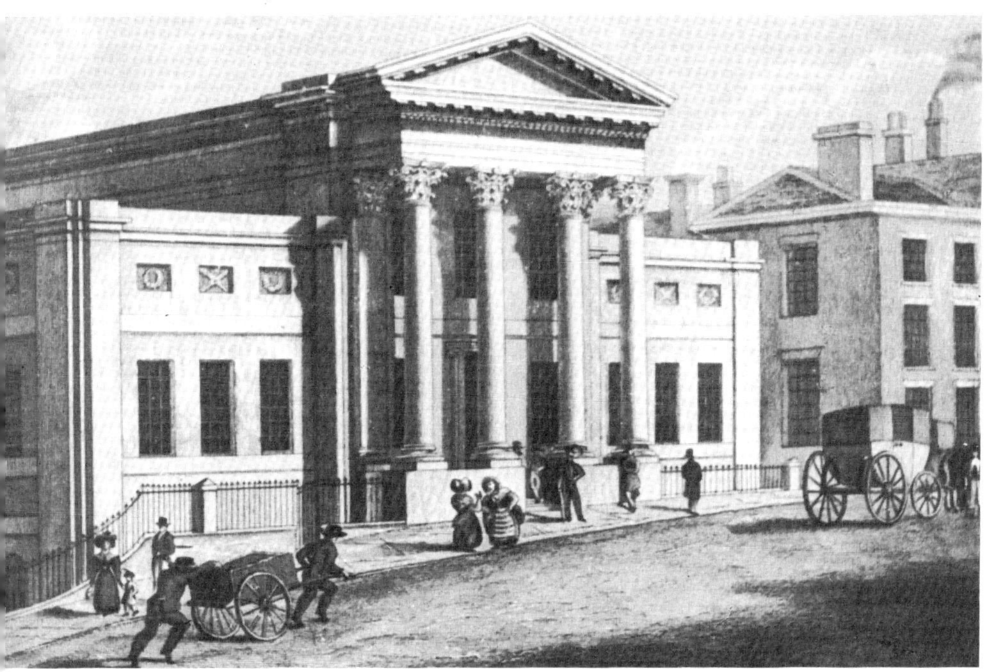

30. Leeds Court House, which contained a prison in the basement.

high and it needed little provocation to spark off an explosion of violence. In August the Plug Riots began and according to Ben Travis in his *History of Todmorden* they had their origin amongst the weavers of Thomas Bayley and Sons at Stalybridge in Lancashire. A woman weaver went to see one of the young masters about a grievance and during a heated argument he rashly said that he would make the weavers glad to work a day for one of the cabbages in his garden. Returning to the loom cellar she told the other weavers what had been said and the news spread like wildfire. Before 10 a.m. on this day, 2 August, all the cotton-mills in the town had the boilers emptied by drawing the plugs and the mills were at a standstill. Weavers in neighbouring towns followed suit and on Friday 12 August 1842 thousands of Lancashire cotton workers poured over the Pennines into Yorkshire to stop work in the Yorkshire mills, which they did by raking out the fires and drawing the boiler plugs and in some cases by emptying the dams. Boilers were plugged at Holmfirth, Honley, Meltham Mills, Armitage Bridge and Marsden. In the Colne Valley the mills of half a dozen townships were brought to a standstill, until at last the mob of over five thousand came to Longroyd Bridge, where the Riot Act was read and a troop of the 4th Lancers dispersed them.

On 17 August a large mob took to the road from Bradford to Leeds. They stopped mills working at Stanningley, Bramley and Fulneck, then divided into parties and went to mills in the surrounding districts, including Armley, Wortley and Farnley, which were forced to close. At Hunslet a large mob turned out the workers at Petty's potteries and then closed mills on the way to Holbeck, where they forced the doors of Marshall's new mill which was defended by the owner and some of his workmen. While the mob was busy in Water Lane the Lancers, under the command of H.R.H. Prince George, galloped up at full speed and formed in line. The Riot Act was read and a few ringleaders were arrested. Victoria Bridge was controlled by a party of Lancers, a party of Fusiliers, and a body of Yorkshire Hussars commanded by Colonel Beckett, together with a body of police headed by magistrates. There were several clashes during the day and many arrests were made. The prisoners were tried at York on 3 September when, considering the circumstances, sentences of up to eighteen months' imprisonment were surprisingly light. Leeds had been well guarded. Apart from the troops stationed in the town, there was a large force of police and special constables, for whom 30,000 staves had been made.

Major-general Sir Charles Napier, who had been given the command of the Northern District in 1839, handled the situation with commendable firmness and sensitivity. Nevertheless, the soldiers were not popular, and in December a complaint from Huddersfield said: 'We have been saddled with the presence and expense of a detachment of the 32nd Foot (which however the Town never needed, being perfectly quiet) who have at times behaved themselves in a most disgraceful manner'.

By an Act of 1704 a West Riding Registry of Deeds had been established at Wakefield, under the supervision of a paid Registrar who was elected by the £100 freeholders of the Riding (all whose freehold property was worth £100 or more each year). This was a lucrative sinecure and it was fought for at times with all the vigour of a General Election. The election held in November, caused by the death of W. F. L. Scott, was preceded by an intensive canvass of all the gentry, merchants and manufacturers who were qualified to vote. The candidates were T. B. Hodgson, Esq. of Skelton, near York, the Hon. Arthur Lascelles of Harewood, and James Stephenson, Esq., a barrister of London. Mr Stephenson took no steps to promote his candidature, so the contest lay between Hodgson and Lascelles. Mr Lascelles had powerful political support: his brother, the Hon. Edwin Lascelles, was Chairman of the West Riding magistrates, who were responsible for the election. Mr Hodgson numbered among his supporters the Duke of Norfolk, Earl Fitzwilliam, Sir F. L. Wood, Mr Fawkes of Farnley, Lord Hawke,

WAKEFIELD

**SOKE.**

***Fellow Townsmen,***

In the present triumphant State of liberal feeling, is it not possible to adopt means by which that greatest of all our evils can be removed?

**Our exertions, Fellow Townsmen, have been most actively aroused for a cause, of itself, of no value; surely a question which *every moment* oppresses both us and our children, ought not to be longer neglected.**

**Let a MEETING BE CALLED,—let Plans be organized,—and Subscriptions set on foot, which will *most certainly* secure the choice of buying *cheap bread* where we please.**

**A Townsman.**

31. The Soke of Wakefield. Ancient rights and customs frequently impeded modern developments, as is illustrated by this hand-bill.

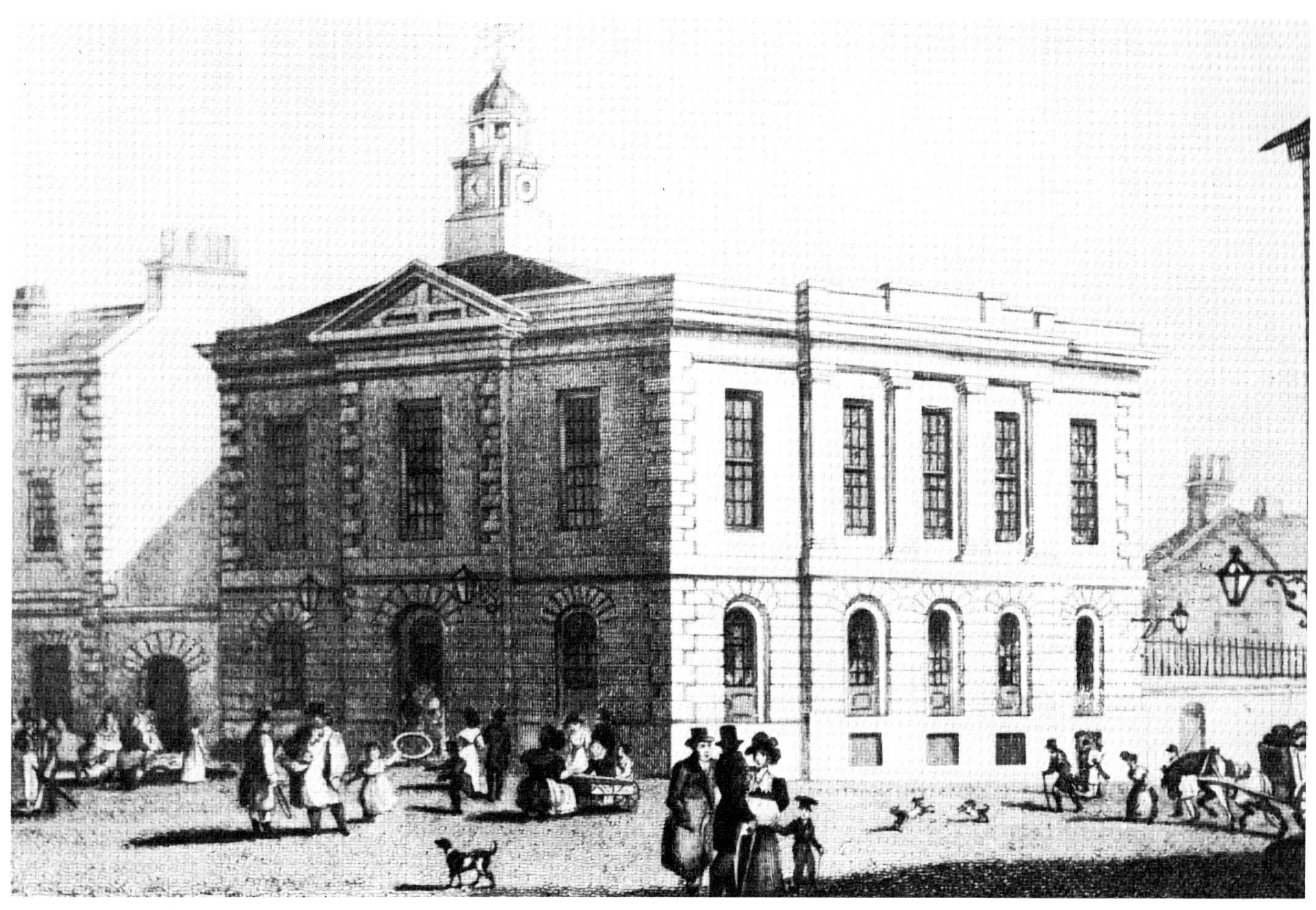

32. The Town Hall, Sheffield, which also housed a local gaol.

Mr George Lane Fox, Mr F. Wilson, and Sir George Armitage, Bt.

Agents were appointed by the candidates for each area of the county and they were urged to form committees to canvass the voters, provide transport and any necessary refreshment. At Barnsley, Mr Hodgson's agent was a solicitor, Mr George Keir, who set up his committee room at a public house there. He was instructed to consider what conveyances he could get in his district and bespeak the conveyances should they be required, if necessary retaining innkeepers and proprietors to keep them exclusively for him and, if required, to pay them a small fee for this purpose. A postscript to his instructions read: 'Wherever we can make the railway available we shall, and the conveyances would, in such cases, have to go to the nearest railway station'. The canvass was carried out with vigour, and excuses such as that of John Wilcock of Cawthorne that he only kept one horse 'and he is in Physic', or of William Jackson of Gawber Hall Old Colliery that he was ill and could only now sit up as he had 'had foure blistering plasters on for foure days', were not allowed to prevent them being transported to Wakefield in special coaches.

The election began on 22 November and lasted for three days. The weather was bad and travelling difficult but the *Leeds Mercury* reported that there had been:

> . . . few occasions in which Wakefield presented a scene of greater animation than on Tuesday last, and especially when so large a number of £100 freeholders were present at one time. The streets throughout the town wore all the aspects of bustle and excitement which generally characterize Wakefield on the days of a warmly contested West Riding Parliamentary Election.

Proceedings were opened at the West Riding Court House when the Chairman of the magistrates vacated the chair because of his kinship with Arthur Lascelles, and five magistrates were elected to supervise the election. The meeting then adjourned to the Corn Exchange where booths had been erected and provision made for accommodating magistrates and lawyers. There was no secret ballot and the state of the poll was declared frequently throughout the day.

The election was one of the most exciting ever witnessed. On the first day the pressure of voters broke

THE NEW

**"House that Jack Built,"**

*HUMBLY DEDICATED TO*

**MR. JOHN MARSHALL,**

***FLAX SPINNER, HOLBECK.***

This is the House that Jack Built.

This is the Flax all heckled and torn, that lays in the House that Jack built.

These are the Children all forlorn, who toil and slave from night till morn, in spinning the Flax, all heckled and torn, that lays in the House that Jack built.

This is the Man all ***shaven and shorn***, for whom the poor Children all forlorn, toil and slave from night till morn, in spinning the Flax, all heckled and torn, that lays in the House that Jack built,

This is John Bull, a Freeman born, whom the Man with his head all shaven and shorn, thinks to lead by the nose, by talking of Corn, while the poor Children all forlorn, get so little for toiling from night till morn, in spinning his Flax, all heckled and torn, that lays in the House that Jack built.

This is the *Lord* so very high-born, who treated his LONG WOOL friends with scorn, yet has joined with the Man all shaven and shorn, to lead John Bull by the nose, by ***talking*** of Corn, but if they don't mind they'll be tossed and torn, or be sent with the Children all forlorn, to twist from the Flax, all heckled and torn, a Rope for to hang themselves some morn, in front of

THE HOUSE THAT JACK BUILT.

WALLER, PRINTER, WAKEFIELD.

33. The House that Jack Built: a reminder of the Corn Laws controversy.

34. Election of the West Riding Registrar. A copy letter sent to Mr William Jackson of Gawber Colliery, near Barnsley, in November 1842.

Dear Sir,

Mr Keir will call upon you with a Chaise at 8 o'Clock in the Morning and I hope and trust you will be well enough to come down here to Breakfast & go in a covered Carriage to Wakefield – Mr Hodgson cannot afford to lose one Vote and every attention shall be paid to your comfort & convenience

Yours truly

Geo: [illegible]

Wednesday Night

Mr Wm Jackson

the barriers, and amidst the confusion tables were overturned and broken. During all the babel of confusion the crier of the court announced at the top of his powerful voice: 'Gentlemen, take care of your pockets; there are pickpockets in the room, one gentleman has had his pocket picked of a purse containing thirteen sovereigns and another has had his pocket book taken'. This added to the confusion as voters in the midst of the throng tried to check their wallets and in some cases to pass them to friends on the fringe for safe custody. It was some time before order was restored.

At the end of the first day Mr Lascelles was leading by 258 votes; on the second day his lead was reduced to 77; and for most of the third day it was neck and neck. Half an hour before closing time on the third day a special train arrived along the recently-constructed railway, bringing seventeen voters for Mr Hodgson from Sheffield, an event which was compared with the arrival of Blücher and his troops on the field of Waterloo. The final count was Hodgson 1,712, Lascelles 1,680 – Hodgson was in by 32 votes. Lascelles's disconcerted supporters left the town, and the victory dinner which they had prepared was enjoyed by the exuberant supporters of Hodgson.

As usual the newspapers had the last word : 'The result will on many accounts be very far from agreeable to the House of Harewood, and it will not add to the harmony of the Tory party in the West Riding'.

## 6. Religion and education

The West Riding had a strong tradition of vigorous nonconformity, and chapels of the various dissenting groups were found throughout the county. Many of the leading public men were nonconformists, notable among them Edward Baines, editor of the *Leeds Mercury*. The chapels played a prominent part in the life of the communities and preserved and developed the self-respect of the working population.

In Leeds, besides the places of worship of the Church of England, there were found the following chapels: 7 Wesleyan Methodist, 3 New Connexion Methodist, 4 Association Methodist, 3 Primitive Methodist, 1 Quaker, 2 Roman Catholic, 8 Independent, 1 Baptist, 1 Unitarian, 1 Arian, 1 Inghamite, 1 Southcotarian, 1 Swedenborgian, 1 Jewish (no regular place of worship). These thirty-five chapels provided a total of 30,596 seats. In addition the Moravian bishop, the Rev. John Holmes, lived at Fulneck, near Pudsey, and his small community made its mark on the life of the neighbourhood.

Leeds, Bradford and Barnsley had communities of Roman Catholics which were expanded each year by the influx of Irish immigrants. There was one church at Barnsley and one at Bradford. The Catholic clergy were much concerned with assisting their people to adapt to the new social conditions in England, but they discouraged them from joining the trade unions and friendly societies, as some of these had secret rituals which the Church considered harmful to the development of true religion.

35. Edward Baines, editor of the *Leeds Mercury*, a notable politician in 1842.

36. The Wesley Chapel, Halifax which was claimed 'not to be surpassed by any chapel belonging to that denomination of Christians in the West Riding'. The cost of building was £4,000.

Almost everywhere there was dissension and suspicion between the various Churches, and this was often a stumbling-block to progress, especially as regards education. As Sir James Graham wrote, 'Religion, the keystone of education, is in this country the bar to its progress'. The nonconformists, indeed, had only been allowed full civil rights since 1828, and the Roman Catholics since 1829. Besides the accepted religious organizations, a new Society of Rational Religionists had developed and its missioners were busy in the West Riding, organizing public meetings in the major towns.

The Church of England, with its centuries-old system of organization, was at first slow to adapt to the changes brought about by the Industrial Revolution. The parochial system had been adequate for the pastoral care of rural communities, but the growth of population in the industrial areas destroyed the personal association of priest and people. There was also an acute shortage of churches in the towns. This was already evident after the Napoleonic wars, when Parliament granted £1 million for the erection of new churches, many of which were built in the West Riding.

In an attempt to improve the situation the Diocese of Ripon was created in 1836, with Charles Thomas Longley, a former Headmaster of Harrow, as Bishop. This was the first new diocese to be formed in England since the Reformation. Within it lay the industrial areas of the Aire and Calder Valleys, and steps were taken to bring new life to the churches there. The Society for the Increase of Church Accommodation, formed at a meeting in Wakefield in September 1838, was followed in December 1841 by a further meeting there, when the Ripon Diocesan Board of Education was established, and in 1842 the Church, concerned at the lack of proper training for teachers, initiated a Diocesan Training School for the York and Ripon Dioceses, in Monkgate, York.

In Sheffield, where four new churches had been built from the Million Pound Fund, the vicar of Sheffield was still solely responsible for the cure of a hundred thousand souls. Halifax, which included twenty-three townships, was believed to be the largest parish in

England, covering 75,740 acres. New ideas about the rôle of the Church in society and standards of pastoral care brought a response from such distinguished churchmen as the Rev. W. F. Hook, DD, Vicar of Leeds, whose work in that city received widespread commendation and provided a pattern for reorganization elsewhere in the country.

New churches were built in populous areas, and on 8 February the Bishop of Ripon consecrated St John's church at Bowling, built at the expense of the Bowling Iron Works. In the following July the Archbishop of York consecrated a church and cemetery at Ardsley, near Barnsley, and conducted a Confirmation service there on the same day.

It was possible to obtain the exclusive use of a pew in a church by the payment of a pew rent. This system ensured that the best pews went to the middle and upper classes. The practice was very unpopular and care was taken to secure large numbers of free pews in the new churches.

An interesting religious character living in the West Riding was John Wroe, who was born at Bowling, Bradford, in 1782 and resided for many years near Wakefield. He claimed to have seen visions and that he was divinely inspired. He was accepted as the successor of Joanna Southcott, who had declared herself a prophetess, and from then onwards he adopted the title of 'prophet'. At some of his meetings he was attended by twelve virgins dressed in white robes, but he was not always well received and as early as 1831 he was driven out of Bradford by an angry mob.

'I can't read; I have never been to school, . . . I

37. The interior of Leeds Parish Church of St Peter. The church had been rebuilt under the supervision of R. D. Chantrell, architect, at a cost of £29,770 6*s*. 8*d*., which was raised by voluntary subscription. It was reopened for worship on 2 September 1841. There were 3,000 sittings of which 1,800 were free.

38. The interior of Halifax Parish Church. Halifax Choral Society had such a fine reputation that Mendelssohn specially dedicated to the Society his setting of the 114th Psalm, which was first sung by the Society in the Parish Church in 1842.

think God made the world, but I don't know where God is. I never heard of Jesus Christ.' The speaker was Eliza Coats, aged eleven years, the date 1841. Her words, published in 1842, emphasized the need for universal compulsory elementary education. Eliza was not alone in her ignorance, for she was one of thousands of children who had little or no schooling. It was not that schools did not exist, for there were in the county ancient grammar schools, endowed schools, National schools, Lancasterian schools and private schools, day and boarding. Yet if all the children had gone to school there would not have been sufficient places for them – not surprising since the schools depended on private charity to provide and maintain them.

Since 1833 the Government had made a grant to promote the education of the workers' children. This was used for the provision of new schools, but the sponsors had to raise a substantial part of the cost before a grant was allowed, and the Government money was, in effect, shared by the National and Lancasterian Societies. These two societies were the main providers of schools during the first half of the nineteenth century. The National Society owed its origin to Dr Andrew Bell, and aimed at promoting the doctrine of the Church of England. His method of teaching, known as the monitorial system, was cheap and mechanical: the teacher taught a few boys and they, in turn, instructed the others. Joseph Lancaster, after whom the other society was named, had similar ideas, but believed that religious education should be non-denominational. The general policy of these schools was to take in children at the age of six, although

39. St John's Church-in-the-Wilderness. Built in the wilds of Turvin Vale, this church catered for a widely scattered population. A contemporary writer described the children as ragged and dirty, running about the roadside as if they belonged to nobody, and the men as brutal and uncouth, while 'the women, likewise, are unwomanly in their appearance, reminding one of the sexless witches in *Macbeth*'. He concluded his unflattering description by saying: 'if no-one else will care for these wild children of the wilderness, we, of the Church, will care for them, and be unto them even as a mother to her little ones'.

40. The Parish Day School, Hartshead, was situated in the churchyard and was endowed by the Armytage family of Kirklees Hall for the education of eighteen poor children. The Rev. Patrick Brontë, father of the famous Brontë sisters, was vicar of this parish from 1810 to 1815.

age limits varied locally. The average time spent at school was two years.

Pupils took their 'school pence' along each week. At the Barnsley National schools, with 160 pupils enrolled, the average payment was $1\frac{1}{2}d.$ each week per pupil, for which sum they were taught reading, writing, grammar and arithmetic. The boys outnumbered the girls by 120 to 40. In the same town the new St George's National school charged 3*d.* for those above eight years of age and 2*d.* for those under. The subjects taught were scripture, reading, writing, arithmetic and sewing. Out of a total of 440 pupils attending six schools, 288 were able to read and 189 could write. Each day one pupil in five was absent.

Younger children might attend dame schools where they could learn spelling, reading and, in some cases, sewing. These were usually small schools of varying quality: some were little more than child-minding establishments; others, particularly those under the control of religious bodies, appear to have been more efficient. The Roman Catholics had a school at Peas Hill, Barnsley, with 44 boys and 7 girls, each of whom paid 6*d.* a week.

Many children learnt to read and write in Sunday schools, and for some this was the only education they received. In Barnsley 2,456 children attended Sunday schools: of these, 787 attended Church Sunday schools, and the remaining 1,669 attended 'dissenting schools', including 130 Roman Catholics and 166 who attended the Odd Fellows' Sunday School, where there was no religious instruction.

Keighley, with a population of 13,412 and woollen-, cotton- and paper-mills, provided an example of the range of schools to be found in industrial communities. There were several endowed schools, a National School (1825), and a Mechanics' Institute. The Free School, founded in 1713, had an endowment of £162 per annum and was free to parishioners for tuition in English as well as Latin and Greek. There was a preparatory school, founded in 1716 and endowed with £40 per annum, and also the Hare-hills Free School with an endowment of about £38 per annum.

There were many good grammar schools in the West Riding but the number of children attending them was relatively small. Leeds Grammar School, with the Rev. Joseph Holmes, DD, as headmaster, had 24 pupils in the upper school, 40 in the middle, and 49 in the lower, which made a total of 113 on the roll. The curriculum of these schools was traditional, and demand for an education including more 'useful' subjects was met to some extent by private academies. At Sheffield a private school offered Latin, Greek, French, commercial subjects, stenography, book-keeping, mathematics and land surveying. Pens, ink and the use of books cost an additional penny per week. This school also provided evening instruction in many subjects on Mondays, Wednesdays and Fridays for 8*d.* per week.

Boarding schools varied in quality from the likes of Dotheboys' Hall in Charles Dickens's *Nicholas Nickleby*, which was based on a school he visited near Bowes, to the excellence of the Quaker school at Ackworth and the Moravian school at Fulneck, amongst whose distinguished 'old boys' were Richard Oastler and the Sheffield poet, James Montgomery.

Eastfield House, Doncaster, built as an additional stand for the race-course, was now a school for deaf and dumb children. Under the control of the Yorkshire Institution for the Instruction of Deaf and Dumb Children, it admitted children between the ages of eight and fourteen years of age. The course, based on Pestalozzian principles, lasted five years. Boys were given additional training in mechanical subjects, and girls received tuition in household work. The cost to a poor family was 2*s.* 6*d.* a week; others paid £20 a year, and some pupils were admitted from other counties for a small additional charge.

Mechanics' institutes, which provided lectures in technical and scientific subjects, were to be found in most towns. In 1837 the Yorkshire Union of Mechanics' Institutes was formed, the first of such organizations in the country. Reading-rooms were provided, but in some places restrictions were placed on the type of book considered suitable. In 1839 the secretary of the Sheffield Institute had been expelled for admitting 'subversive books', but he went on to play a leading part in the establishment of a 'Hall of Science' in that

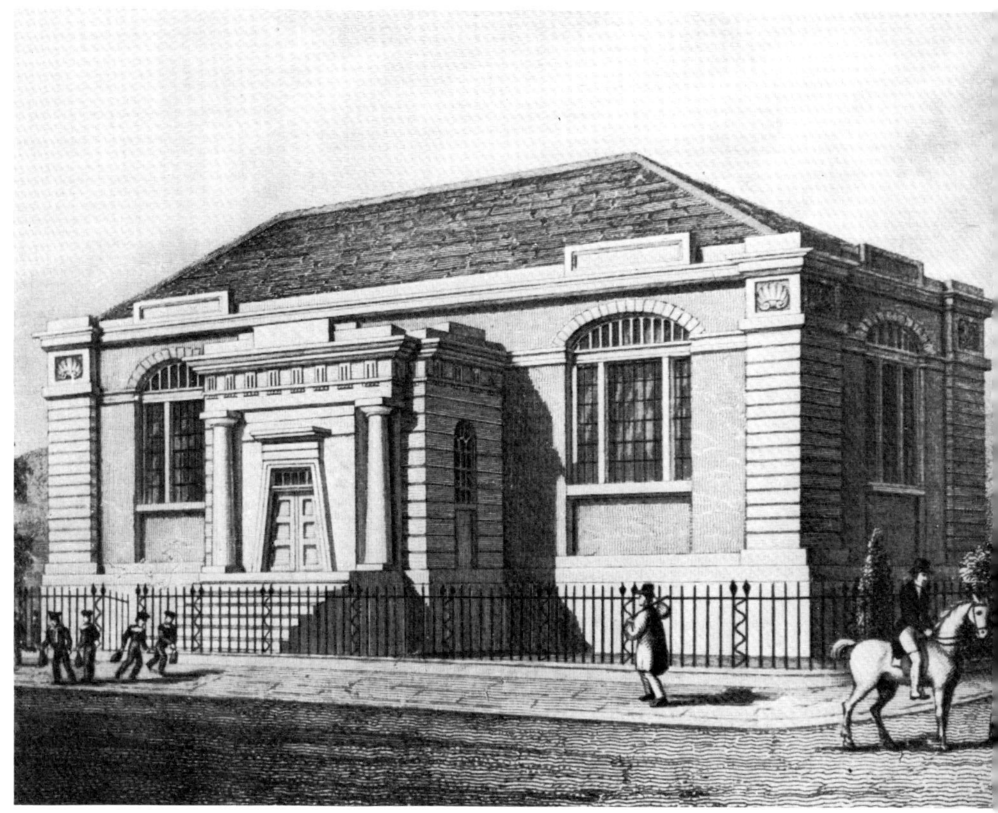

41. Bradford Grammar School, one of the twelve schools which had the privilege of sending candidates for Lady Hastings's Exhibitions at Queen's College, Oxford. In 1842 the Rev. Samuel Slack, MA, was headmaster.

42. The West Riding Proprietary School, Wakefield, founded by the issue of 300 shares of a total value of £7,500; this school was opened on 6 August 1834. In 1842 the Rev. Samuel Fennell, DD, was headmaster, and the fees were £10 per annum, entrance fee for library £1, board £35 per annum, drawing £3 extra, and other accomplishments as required.

town. Other voluntary associations encouraged the study of specific branches of knowledge. Amongst these were the Yorkshire Geological Society and the Leeds Literary Society; the latter amalgamated with the Mechanics' Institute in 1842.

An important development was the foundation of the People's College in Sheffield in 1842 – the first of its kind in the country. It grew from the Rev. R. S. Bayley's work at the Sheffield Mechanics' Institute and provided a means of further education for workmen, who could attend lectures in a variety of subjects, before and after work.

Improvements in printing, better communications and the spread of literacy encouraged the production of newspapers. In the West Riding the principal papers were the *Leeds Conservative Journal*, *Leeds Intelligencer*, *Leeds Times*, *Leeds Mercury*, *Bradford Journal*, *Sheffield Mercury*, *Sheffield Independent*, *Yorkshire Gazette*, *Halifax Guardian* and *West Riding Herald*.

Mudie's Circulating Library was advertised in the local press. The Leeds Library, founded in 1768, had one of the most valuable collections of books in the north of England. In Morley the first public library in the town had been founded by a group of public-spirited men of all parties and denominations; this was the first instance of a voluntary association for literary purposes there. An indication of the importance of a local library to the reading public may be judged from the fact that Charlotte Brontë on a visit home would walk specially to Keighley to see if any new books had been added to the library while she had been away.

The remarkable Brontë sisters were very interested in education and during 1842 Charlotte and Emily spent some time in Belgium to gain experience for opening a school in England. Their sister Anne worked as a governess, and brother Branwell, the black sheep of the family, had worked as a clerk for the Manchester to Leeds Railway Company. At Christmas 1842 they were all together again with their father, the Rev. Patrick Brontë, at Haworth Parsonage. Branwell was to begin the new year as a tutor in a private household. A private tutor was a luxury reserved for the upper and middle classes – for the poor there were only the ill-equipped elementary schools.

# 7. Town life

During 1842 a severe trade depression brought grave poverty and hardship to the West Riding of Yorkshire. In the *Fleet Papers* dated 29 January, Oastler mentioned a letter from a friend in the Huddersfield district, who had written:

It is impossible to describe the present state of society in this neighbourhood – it would take me a week to give you an outline of it. If you can form any idea from its being one person's work to give answers to beggars, nearly all the day long, at your door; . . . with thefts, robberies, forgeries, swindlings, deceptions, and cheatings of every description; suicides, starvation, and premature deaths for want of proper food and attention; with roads infested with beggars, six or eight in a lot, asking, 'Can you bestow your charity on a lump of us that are out o' work?' . . . We have thought things bad before, but never anything equal to the present state of things.

At Wakefield a Mendicity Society had been formed to safeguard the benevolent from distributing their alms haphazardly. Sympathizers were asked to purchase tickets at three for one shilling, and to give one ticket to any pauper they wished to help. Each ticket could be exchanged for one pound of bread and one pint of soup. Members of the Wakefield Benevolent Society visited the homes of the poor and did their best to make good the shortage of blankets. Elsewhere individual philanthropists tried to help, as at Snapethorpe where a Mr Lock donated twelve cartloads of coal for the poor.

At Barnsley a public subscription was raised and sufficient money collected to supply food for 3,000 individuals for several months. Four tons of oatmeal and fifty tons of potatoes were dispensed during this period. A report from Dewsbury said that where a few months previously there had been no pawn-shops, now there were two. During January, February and March 4,000 families, comprising upwards of 16,000 indivi-

43. Crown Street, Halifax: a typical street scene.

44. Commercial Buildings, Leeds. These magnificent buildings, which contained a large newsroom, testified to the growth and importance of Leeds as a commercial centre. They were completed in 1829 at a cost of nearly £35,000. The Yorkshire District Bank, seen on the right, was opened seven years later.

duals, were on the books of the Leeds workhouse as receiving parochial aid, in addition to which 10,000 persons had been recipients from the Relief Fund of £7,000 raised by voluntary subscriptions. The paupers had been given work breaking stones, but by August, when they had broken 150,000 tons, it was decided to pay them 6*s.* a week for not breaking stones rather than pay them 7*s.* 6*d.* for doing so. The Poor Rate in Leeds had then increased fifty per cent; and the Manufacturers' Relief Committee in London had sent £500 to the Committee for the Relief of the Poor in Leeds. The latter committee had been formed in January, when it was estimated that there were 7,304 persons living in the town on an income of 1*s.* 7⅛*d.* per week.

In Sheffield an application was made for aid from the General Relief Fund, which had been raised throughout the country on the authority of the Queen's Letter. It was then estimated that 3,000 men and 1,500 women were unemployed, of which number 2,000 men alone were receiving parochial aid. In almost every industrial town the pattern was the same, poverty and despair hanging over them like a dark cloud.

Steps were being taken to solve some of the problems created by large urban communities. The Report from the Select Committee on the Health in Towns had presented a depressing picture of the housing and sanitary conditions in the five major towns, including Leeds, which had nearly doubled their population in thirty years. The existing local government services were inadequate, and were overwhelmed by the magnitude of the problem. Bad sanitation was all the more serious because of overcrowded conditions in working-class areas. In Boot and Shoe Yard, Leeds, 340 persons lived in fifty-seven rooms, for which they paid a total annual rent of £214. There were three out-offices (privies), from one of which, during the period of cholera, seventy-five cart-loads of soil were removed by order of the Commissioners. It had not been cleaned out again. There was no water supply within a quarter of a mile, and very few of the inhabitants possessed vessels suitable for holding water. The Yard terminated in a cul-de-sac, so there was no through passage of air, with the result that cases of malignant fever were continually being sent to the fever hospital. In other parts of the town the conveniences outside the public houses were exposed to public view, streets were obstructed by clothes-lines, and cellars and steps were unprotected. The North East Ward, in which out of 16,269 inhabitants 15,399 were working-class, was described as 'having dangerous excavations, bad drainage, little or no sewerage, here and there pieces of stagnant water, ash-holes exposed, out-offices without doors or seats'.

Out of a total of 586 streets in Leeds, 276 were so full of lines and linen as to be almost impassable, even to foot passengers. In some streets on the York Road every house had a sump-hole under the cellars, long since stagnant, where regurgitating sewers were a severe hazard to the health of the inhabitants. All the refuse and filth that did not lie stagnant on the roads poured into the River Aire, which had become an open sewer, yet from which the town drew its drinking water. In some areas of the town people were dependent on the hawker's cart for their water supply, and paid as much as two shillings a week for it. The problem of polluted and inadequate water supply faced most large towns. Some reservoirs existed and others were proposed. In 1842 Bradford obtained an Act to bring water from Manywells or Emanuel's Height, Wilsden, to reservoirs at Chellow Dean and Whetley Hill. The Old Waterworks Company was transferred to the Bradford Waterworks Company with a capital of £88,500.

Thirteen out of every seventeen inhabitants of Leeds belonged to the working class. For the poorer of them there was little comfort in the overcrowded houses or rooms they lived in, so some sought warmth and comfort in public houses and spirit shops. In fine weather they enjoyed the open space of Woodhouse Moor, the drainage of which three years earlier had been a means of providing work for the unemployed. Since there were too few houses to accommodate the increased population, the many lodging houses were overcrowded: in some instances there were sixteen people living and sleeping in one room 15 feet by 13 feet, with just one small window. Speculative building flourished. Long rows of workers' cottages were built without any regard for drainage, ventilation or the paving of the streets, though these were wider than the older courts

45. The Shewsbury Hospital and Chapel, Sheffield. With greater concentration of people in the towns, better and larger hospitals were needed. At Sheffield much interest was shown in medical matters, and this hospital, built in 1829, was described as one of the most elegant edifices in this part of the country. It had its own resident chaplain.

46. The Huddersfield and Upper Agbrigg Infirmary. Built in 1830, this hospital served Huddersfield and a wide area of the surrounding countryside. The sum of £1,549 was raised towards the cost of building by the sale of fancy goods donated to a public bazaar.

and alleys. Baths in private houses were almost unknown but some towns had public baths. In Leeds there were two, one of a superior type used by the middle classes, and another, charging a smaller fee, for the poorer townspeople. In this respect Leeds seems to have been better equipped than other large towns.

In many large West Riding towns there were colonies of Irish workers, whose living standards were generally low. In Leeds there were between 4,000 and 5,000 such immigrants and others were to be found in Bradford and Barnsley.

A further hazard to health was the number of overcrowded churchyards in the centres of towns. Already full, these were inadequate for the expanding populations and there was growing awareness that new cemeteries should be opened away from town centres and the sources of water supply. Leeds applied for an Act to authorize this development and on 25 April evidence was given before a Select Committee of the House of Commons that 142,293 corpses were buried in the three parochial burial grounds. On 12 July the Leeds Burial Ground Act was passed in the House of Commons. Similar measures were adopted by other towns.

Although life expectancy was not long, and there was a large infant mortality rate, a few people managed to live beyond the age of eighty, and these rare examples of longevity were duly noted in the press. Medical services were inadequate and of very unequal quality. A common treatment for many ills was bleeding; for this a special instrument called a phleme was used. It consisted of a box containing two or three sharp knives, which was strapped to the wrist. Pulling a lever forced the blades into the wrist and when the approved quantity of blood was let off the wrist was bandaged, the doctor drew his fee and chance decided the fate of the patient. Leeches were used for the same purpose. Medical men were aware of their limitations and in the larger towns, especially in Sheffield and Leeds, much thought was given to improving the practice of medicine and surgery. Charles Waterton, the remarkable squire of Walton Hall, brought back from his wanderings in South America a drug called wourali poison (*curare*). A scratch from an arrow tipped with this poison was sufficient to paralyse a small animal. Waterton interested the doctors of the day by demonstrating its powers and suggested that it could be used in treating hydrophobia.

New industrial diseases were also receiving attention. At Sheffield, 'grinder's asthma', caused by the inhalation of particles of sand and metal, made grinding an unhealthy and short-lived occupation, so attempts were made to draw off the dust as it left the grinding wheel. Any possible remedy was much in demand: the newspapers carried advertisements for such medicines as Perry's Purifying Specific and Mulready's Cough Elixir.

The greater concentration of population and the large number of accidents in industry produced a growing demand for more and better hospitals, as in Leeds, where the Lock hospital was opened at 159, York Street. The plight of the mentally sick was also attracting more attention and by 1842, when the Act for the Inspection of Asylums was passed, the West Riding Pauper Lunatic Asylum at Wakefield had already done much pioneer work in this field. There were several private lunatic asylums, usually called 'retreats', for those who could afford them.

In Barnsley the year 1842 saw the appointment of the first officers under the new Parochial Constables Act. The Chief Constables were John Cordeaux, linen manufacturer, Henry Richardson, linen manufacturer, Thomas Cope, draper, and George Harrison, stationer. Appointed deputies with annual salaries were John Carnelly, £40, George Kershaw, £25, Joseph Winter, £20, and Francis Batty, £5.

Most town centres were well illuminated at nights and there was an ever increasing demand for gas lighting. Bradford Gasworks, which cost £15,000, was opened in 1823, and Pontefract's two gasometers, with a capacity of 5,000 cubic feet, were brought into use in 1832 at a cost of £4,200. However, the candle provided the only light after sundown for many homes, and tallow chandlers continued to do a thriving business.

47. The New Sulphur Spring at Low Harrogate was one of the popular medicinal springs of the period.

Fires were a constant hazard, and in the absence of an efficient fire service the fire brigades were usually owned by an insurance company or a prudent mill-owner. In February there was a fire at the Twelve O'Clock Grinding Wheel in Sheffield; fire-engines were quickly on the scene but 'owing to some unfortunate circumstance' it was three-quarters of an hour

48. The Central Market, Leeds, opened in 1827. This spacious indoor market was divided into three walks with stalls, and a gallery was carried around three sides of the building with a bazaar on one side. The adjacent streets and alleys were occupied by butchers and other traders. Market prices were a guide for prices elsewhere.

before they could play on the flames. In the same month Burton Bridge Mill at Barnsley was destroyed, together with a large quantity of grain and flour. When the mill of Barker and Barwise, between Skipton and Todmorden, caught fire in June, John Fielden and Brothers, of Todmorden, sent their fire-engine with other engines from Burnley to attend the blaze. Sometimes attending the fire was all that they did, for a mill fire was often beyond their capacity to control. In at least one case the fire brigade arrived so drunk that, after the mill had almost burned down, the frustrated workers took over the engine themselves.

In every town market-day brought crowds from the surrounding countryside. On one day in September, 196 carts and waggons and 200 persons with sacks and baskets, brought fruit and vegetables to sell in Wakefield market. Cattle and corn markets flourished in all market towns, and in some towns became major commercial activities. Large indoor markets existed in major towns such as Wakefield, where the Corn Exchange was the largest in the North. The average prices for 1842 were (per quarter); wheat 57*s.* 3*d.*; barley 27*s.* 6*d.*; oats 19*s.* 3*d.*; rye 33*s.*; beans 32*s.* 5*d.*; peas 33*s.* 11*d.* After Smithfield, Wakefield was the largest cattle market in England. On one day in 1842 there were 7,500 sheep and 300 beasts for sale. Beef sold at from 6*s.* to 6*s.* 6*d.* per stone; mutton, clipped, at $5\frac{1}{4}d.$ per pound; mutton, woolled, at 6*d.* to $6\frac{1}{4}d.$ per pound. Apart from the regular markets there were many annual fairs. Barnsley cattle fair was held in February, that of Wakefield in July, when it was reported that the show of cattle was 'very thin, although the horse fair was busier than in former years and three hundred horses were exhibited for sale, but few changed hands'.

In woollen towns cloth was sold in special buildings called 'cloth halls'. These were large imposing structures containing many stalls or rooms. In Bradford many were unoccupied in 1842, as there were fewer individual manufacturers now the mills were becoming mechanized. The cloth markets were usually opened and closed by the ringing of a bell. At Heckmondwike Blanket Market in the last week of March, only one trader answered the call – at Dewsbury, none.

49. Little Westgate, Wakefield. In a period when many people could not read, shop signs were still used, such as the boot in the picture, which was the sign of Speak's Clog Mart. Wooden-soled clogs were normal footwear for mill-girls.

50. Blue Bonnet, the winner of the Great St Leger Stakes at Doncaster in 1842. She was ridden by T. Lye and bred and owned by the Rt. Hon. the Earl of Eglintoun.

# 8. Social life and sport

Fairs and feasts were the highlights of the festive and social life of the towns and villages. Whirligigs, shooting galleries, penny swings, peep-shows, Punch and Judy, conjurors, pea saloons and brandysnap stalls, gambling games and lucky bags, fortune-telling pigs, fat women, eight-legged sheep and other fabulous attractions gathered the whole countryside for a riot of merry-making. For twopence a taste of drama could be enjoyed in performances of *Hamlet*, the *Mirfield Murders*, or some other equally desperate story. As the day wore on, home-brewed beer from the public houses was in heavy demand, and riotous scenes and fights were common. Fairs were held at the same time each year, and for weeks before preparations were made to feed the family and friends expected for a jolly reunion. Children ran out to meet the travelling showmen and escorted them to the fairground, laughing and cheering, helping or hindering. In 1842 this was probably all many of them could do, for the general poverty affected the fair as it did all other activities – a report on Huddersfield Fair remarked: 'It's a grand Fair, this Huddersfield, but folks has gotten na' brass'. Brass or not, the fair often continued long into the night, with dancing and merrymaking which kept the whole town awake.

Walking and running contests and fabulous feats of

skill and endurance, usually for a wager, were major attractions. One of the greatest performers of the day was Mountjoy. It was recorded that on 8 October he 'completed the remarkable feat of walking from Leeds to Bradford and back again three times within fourteen hours on six successive days, being sixty-two miles each day'. Then on 17 October at the Victoria Cricket Ground, Woodhouse Moor, Leeds,

> in the space of half an hour he ran one mile, walked one mile forwards and one backwards – trundled a hoop half a mile – wheeled a barrow half a mile – hopped upon one leg two hundred yards – ran backwards two hundred yards – picked up forty eggs with his mouth, placed a yard apart, without his knees touching the ground or his hands touching the eggs, brought each egg in his mouth, and deposited it in a bucket of water without breaking. After a rest of thirty minutes he ran seven miles and leaped over sixty hurdles at an elevation of nearly four feet, having an egg in his mouth while leaping over the last twenty.

One of the most popular games was Knurr and Spell. There were several methods of playing it. The most common among children was with a 'sendstick' or pommel, and a wooden spell with a hole at one end, in which to place the knurr. The impact of a blow on the spell, at the opposite end to the hole, would pitch the knurr into the air where the player could give it a hearty swipe. Adults used more sophisticated equipment, and sometimes spent hours whittling away a piece of hollywood to produce a knurr to their liking. In May 1842 the game played on Heath Common for £5 a side between Thornhill and Morley ended in a win for Morley by four scores. Some enthusiasts even neglected church-going to enjoy a game. At the Wakefield Petty Sessions in February, Richard Bramhall, John Ramsden and George Whittaker were brought up to answer a charge of playing on the Sabbath. The court was sympathetic and they were each fined one shilling, to pay the constable for his trouble.

51. The grandstand, Doncaster, erected in 1777, the year after the foundation of the St Leger Stakes. In 1825 the races were extended to five days.

Cricket was played on the highways and commons, with a bat curved for hitting rather than defending; bowling was of the under-arm variety. In the absence of a coin for deciding the first innings, one side of a flat stone was wetted by spit 'wet' and 'dry' were called instead of 'heads or tails'. Besides such informal games, selected teams would play for a wager; many

52. The Mansion House and Betting Rooms, Doncaster, centres of social life. In January 1842, a masque ball was held in the Betting Rooms (on the left).

recalled the match played for £50 some years earlier at Kirkstall Bridge between eleven Scientific Players from Sheffield and twenty-two Yorkshire Players. The Sheffield Players won by four runs and nine wickets. The final score was Sheffield 143 for 1, Yorkshire 139 for 21. At the Sheffield and Dalton match played in June at Whitaker Bridge, near Huddersfield, the game ended abruptly because the Sheffield umpire gave a Daltonian 'run out' when he was not. The Sheffield team left without coming to any agreement and the wager was left in the Huddersfield bank, as neither side could draw it until agreement was reached.

In February the members of the Sheffield Skating Club played a cricket match on ice on a pond in the Wardsend estate, the sides being chosen by Messrs Rodgers and Dodworth. The first team scored 128 in two innings, the second 100. During the same week the Sheffield Wednesday Cricket Club held a ball at Hyde Park House. Cricket was obviously very popular there: in the park was a large cricket ground, laid down in 1826 and enclosed by a wall. It had a large stone gallery for spectators. There were several bowling-greens near the Botanical Gardens, also swimming baths, and, in one building, a theatre and circus.

During the winter months concerts and dances were popular entertainments for the middle classes. A public ball was held at Wakefield in January in honour of the christening of Albert Edward, Prince of Wales, when the music was provided by John Yeaman's Quadrille Band. For the Badsworth Hunt Ball, held in Pontefract Town Hall in February, Clegg's Band from Sheffield was engaged. Singing was a traditional and popular pastime, and most towns had a choral society. A choral concert was held at Dewsbury in April. In June, at the Annual Meeting of the Huddersfield Choral Society, it was reported to be in a flourishing and progressive state. Cleckheaton had an Annual Philharmonic Concert, which was held in January.

Bellringing, requiring both skill and stamina, did not lack enthusiasts. On 26 September a prize-ringing took place at Wragby between six bellringers from Barnsley and six from Darfield, for £20. The perfor-

53. In a county latticed with streams and rivers, many country houses had lakes in their grounds suitable for fishing, boating and sailing, such as this one at Cannon Hall, near Barnsley.

54. Theatre bill.

mance consisted of 5,040 changes, which the former completed, the Darfield company having 'got out' in the fourth peal. The Barnsley company were declared the winners. On Monday and Tuesday, 14 and 15 November, a great prize-ringing took place at Barnsley. Fifteen companies of six bellringers from different parts of Yorkshire attended. The prizes for which they competed were four purses of £6, £4, £2 and £1, and were awarded to those who rang the best of 'Three True Treble Peals'. The Barnsley youths welcomed their fellow ringers with three peals, which they executed in a style seldom equalled; after which they took their seats as Censors and the several companies went on in the following order:

| | *Faults* | | *Faults* |
|---|---|---|---|
| High Hoyland | 2,063 | Mirfield | 1,458 |
| Kirkheaton | out | Meltham | 1,489 |
| Wath | 1,271 | Holmfirth | 728 |
| Kirby | out | Darfield | 845 |
| Roystone | 1,617 | Almondbury Juniors | out |
| Darton | 2,240 | Silkstone Seniors | 754 |
| Silkstone Juniors | out | Ecclesfield | out |
| Almondbury Seniors | 1,060 | | |

The Censors, in the presence of the Committee, summed up the numbers of faults, and awarded the prizes as follows: Holmfirth, first prize; Silkstone Seniors, second prize; Darfield, third prize; Almondbury Seniors, fourth prize. Ten shillings each were given to the two companies from Mirfield and Meltham, these

55. The Music Hall, Sheffield, promoted by the Sheffield Choral Society in 1823. Always a town for music, Sheffield had held its first Musical Festival in 1769.

(among those that rang through) having come the farthest distance.

The flourishing Friendly Societies played an important role in the social life of most communities. Particularly active were the Oddfellows, who in some places opened their own halls, as at Todmorden in 1840. On Whit Monday the Order of Ancient Foresters had a splendid procession through Wakefield, followed by a ball at the Music Saloon. It was then claimed that the number of 'courts' connected with this Order was upwards of 1,400 and that there were more than 100,000 members in the country, including many MPs

56. Although the rivers in industrial areas were becoming polluted, fishing was still possible in many places.

and other influential gentlemen. At Dewsbury the Brothers of the Lilley of the Valley Lodge No. 39 of the United Ancient Order of Druids celebrated their twelfth anniversary in 1842.

Many of these societies provided some form of relief to their members in times of sickness and adversity, and 1842, when subscription income was down and claims were many, was a difficult year for them. They did, however, bring people together with shared responsibility and gave a sense of self-respect and dignity to those who held office in the various lodges and courts. The Meltham Mills Co-operative Society was established in 1827, and it commenced paying dividends on the amount of members' purchases. It was probably the first society in the land to adopt this practice.

For those who could give, philanthropy was a public duty, and many charitable societies brought people together to further a common cause. Animals were not forgotten, for in 1842 the Wakefield Humanity Society raised funds for the supply of troughs and pipes to provide water for the cattle at the fair.

Gardeners came together at exhibition times and at the Barnsley Horticultural Exhibition in September they competed for a silver cup and various other prizes. Plants of outstanding size attracted much attention and in November a mammoth gourd (described as *Cucurbita maxime Papo*) was cut in the grounds of John Birks, Esq. of Hemingfield. Its horizontal circumference was 5 feet $5\frac{3}{4}$ inches, its diameter 1 foot $10\frac{1}{2}$ inches, and its height 1 foot $4\frac{1}{2}$ inches. The plant covered a space of 9 yards by 8 yards and weighed 6 stones 10 pounds.

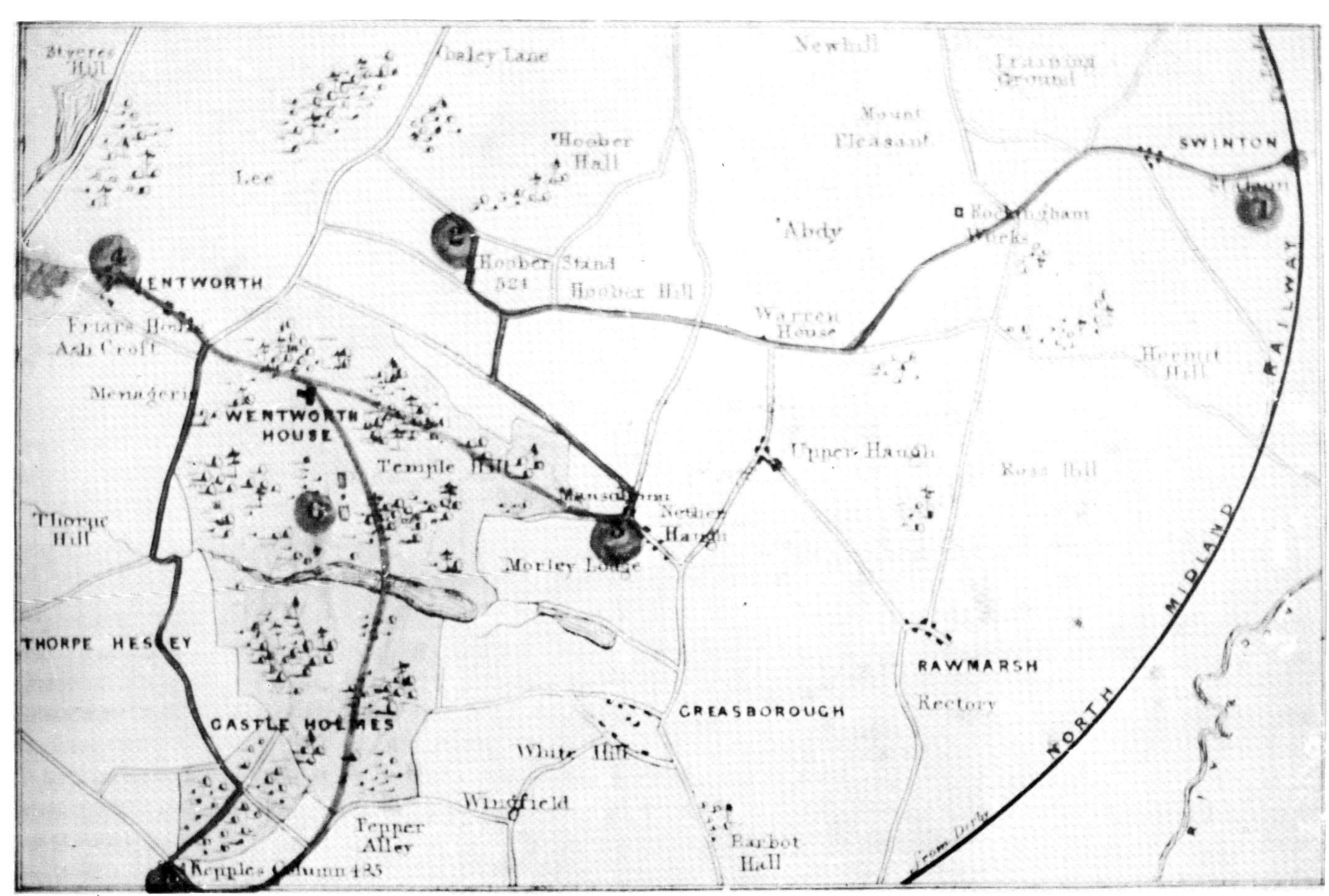


57. Walks and picnics were a common form of recreation and pleasure for all classes of society. Development of the railways widened the scope of such outings. Here is the plan of a proposed visit to Wentworth House.

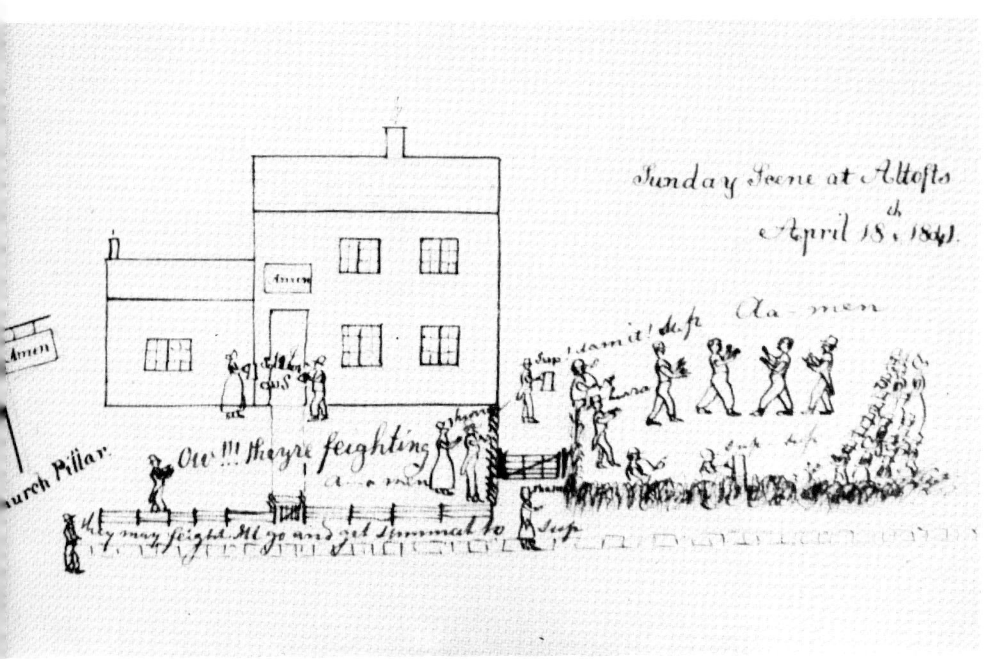


58. This quaint drawing from the inside cover of a school register records the schoolmaster's impression of village life on a Sunday morning.

In some places there were 'under-cover' pigeon-shooting matches. A contemporary report of one such event suggested: 'No doubt the great bulk of birds were obtained by midnight depredations on the pigeon cotes of the surrounding districts.'

Despite the trade depression attempts were made to encourage the thrifty to save: there were savings banks in many towns. It was, in fact, a great age for clubs and societies. People found in these artificial groupings some of the companionship they had lost in moving away from the small agricultural communities to the more anonymous life of industrial areas. These clubs were of almost endless variety: Henpecked Husbands' Societies, Emigration Clubs, Temperance Societies, and, inevitably, clubs and meetings for religious and political purposes.

Picnics and outings were favourite family recreations, and the new railways enabled people to travel farther afield. These were undoubtedly a great attraction in themselves, for in 1842 the Manchester to Leeds Railway carried well over a million passengers.

An eating competition was one of the less edifying pastimes. At Morley Feast a prize was given to the person who could most speedily consume a basin or plate of hot 'hasty pudding' or 'lumpy dicks', as the case might be, using the hands as ladles. A man known as the 'King of Eaters', who lived in Turvin Vale, was noted by a contemporary writer describing life in the area:

> They pride themselves, indeed, upon their gastronomical prowess; and it is no uncommon thing for them to wager that they will eat so many pounds of flesh and potatoes, and drink so many quarts of ale, in a given time. There is one man in this neighbourhood, who is well-known as the King of Eaters and the gastronomic conqueror of all other men. If I were to relate the stories I have heard about this wild cannibal of a man, they would scarcely be credited; although I had them on good authority; eye witnesses, indeed, of the foul orgies they described to me.

Interestingly, a Mr Beard was advertising for capitalists to purchase the use of the Daguerreotype apparatus for forming pictures in miniature. In 1842 there was certainly plenty of scope for this new art of photography.

# Further Reading

Baines, E., *The life of Edward Baines* (Longman, Brown, Green, Longmans, 1851).

Baines, Thomas, *Yorkshire, past and present* (Wm Mackenzie, 1870).

Beresford, M. W. and Jones, G. R. J., *Leeds and its region* (British Assoc. for the Advancement of Science, 1967).

Bradley, Tom, *Old coaching days in Yorkshire* (Yorkshire Conservative Newspaper, 1889).

Select committee on the health of towns, *Report* (1840).

Crabtree, John, *Concise history of the parish and vicarage of Halifax* (Hartley & Walker, 1836).

Cudworth, W., *Round about Bradford* (Thomas Brear, 1876).

Fay, C. R., *Life and labour in the nineteenth century* (Cambridge University Press, 1920).

Grabham, O., *Yorkshire potteries* (S.R. Publishers Ltd reprint, 1971).

Guest, J., *Rotherham pamphlets* (A. Gilling, 1866).

Hadfield, Charles, *British canals* (1950; David & Charles reprint 1973).

Head, Sir G., *A home tour through the manufacturing districts of England* (1835; F. Cass reprint, 1968).

Hobson, R., *Charles Waterton, his home, habits and handiwork* (Whittaker & Co., 1866).

James, J., *History of the worsted manufacture in England* (1857; F. Cass reprint, 1968).

Jubb, S., *History of the shoddy trade* (Houlston & Wright, 1860).

Machin, Frank, *The Yorkshire miners*, Vol. I (National Union of Mineworkers, 1958).

Marshall, John, *The Lancashire and Yorkshire Railway*, Vols I, II, III (David & Charles, 1969–72).

Mayhall, J., *Annals of Leeds and the surrounding districts* (Joseph Johnson, 1860).

Oastler, Richard, *The Fleet Papers, 1841–1844* (Greenwood Reprint Corporation, N.Y., 1968)

Ogden, John, *Yorkshire's river of industry: the story of the River Calder* (Terence Dalton Ltd, 1972).

Priestley, Joseph, *Navigable rivers and canals* (1831; David & Charles reprint, 1969).

Raistrick, A., *West Riding of Yorkshire* (Hodder & Stoughton, 1970).

Rimmer, W. G., *Marshalls of Leeds, flax spinners, 1788–1886* (Cambridge University Press, 1960).

Children's employment commission, *First report: mines* (1842).

Singleton, F., *Industrial revolution in Yorkshire* (Dalesman Publishing Co. Ltd, 1970).

Sykes, D., *History of Huddersfield and the Colne and Holme valleys* (B. Brown & Son)

Tait, A. F., *Views of the Manchester and Leeds Railway* (1845; Frank Graham reprint, 1971).

*Victoria County History of Yorkshire* (3 vols, 1907–25).

Walton, Mary, *Sheffield: its story and its achievements* (1948; S. R. Publishers Ltd reprint, 1968).

White, W., *West Riding Yorkshire Directory* (1842).

## Places to visit

Cannon Hall Art Gallery and Museum, Cawthorne, near Barnsley.

Batley-Bagshaw Museum, Wilton Park (textiles).

Bradford Art Gallery and Museum, Cartwright Hall.

Bradford Industrial Museum, Moorside Mills, Eccleshill (to be opened early summer, 1974).

Cusworth Hall, near Doncaster. South Yorkshire Industrial Museum (crafts and industries; industrial manuscript collection).

Dewsbury Museum and Art Gallery, Crow Nest Park.
Doncaster Museum and Art Gallery, Chequer Road.
Halifax. Bankfield Museum, Akroyd Park (textiles, textile machinery, costume).
Halifax. Shibden Hall Folk Museum of West Yorkshire (agriculture, coaches, workshops).
Haworth. Brontë Museum, the Old Parsonage.
Huddersfield. Tolson Memorial Museum, Ravensknowle Park (local industries, geology).
Ilkley. Manor House Museum and Art Gallery, Castle Yard.
Keighley. Art Gallery and Museum, Cliffe Castle (reconstructed craft workshops).
Leeds. City Art Gallery, Municipal Buildings (Leeds pottery).
Leeds. City Museum, Municipal Buildings.
Leeds. Kirkstall Abbey House Museum (folk museum, streets and workshops).
Rotherham. Municipal Museum and Art Gallery, Clifton Park (Rockingham porcelain).
Sheffield. City Museum, Weston Park (geology, cutlery).
Sheffield. Abbeydale Industrial Hamlet, Abbeydale Road South (eighteenth-century scythe works).
Sheffield. Shepherd Wheel (a water-powered grinding shop). Apply to City Museum.
Skipton. Craven Museum, High Street.
Wakefield. City Museum, Wood Street (Waterton Natural History Collection. County Gaol relics).
York. Castle Museum, Tower Street (folk museum, reconstructed streets and rooms, crafts, agriculture, toys).
York. Railway Museum.
Harewood House. 8 miles from Leeds.
Nostell Priory, near Wakefield.
Heath Hall, near Wakefield.
Oakwell Hall, Batley (The 'Fieldhead' of Charlotte Brontë's novel *Shirley*).
Middleton Railway Trust, Clayton's Yard, Garnet Road, Middleton, Leeds.
Piece Hall, Halifax (cloth hall).
Marshall's Flax Mill, Holbeck, Leeds (Egyptian style frontage – outside view only).
Crank Mill, Morley (outside view only).
Stanley Aqueduct, near Wakefield (outside view only – river and canal navigation).
Leeds and Liverpool Canal, Five Rise Locks, Bingley (View only). Cruises along this canal are arranged by David Lowe, Ivy Road, Shipley.
Aire and Calder Navigation, Wakefield. Fall Ings Lock. Old headquarters' buildings and warehouse, near Wakefield bridge, now dilapidated.
Hebden Bridge and Heptonstall (good examples of valley settlement and hill village in the Pennines).


## Acknowledgements

We would like to thank the following persons and organisations for allowing us to copy some of their pictures and documents: Leeds City Library, pages 28, 29, 30, 32; Wakefield City Library, pages 35, 37, 58; Yorkshire Archaeological Society, pages 19 (picture 15), 27, 31, 39, 41, 42, 47, 48; Mr John Goodchild, Cusworth Hall Industrial Museum, pages 19 (picture 14), 38, 62; Alex Jackson of Leeds, pages 6, 7, 8, 15, 18, 54, 60; The Rev. Canon H. W. Hodgson, page 43. All the remaining illustrations are from the authors' own collection.